Zend Framework Web Services
A php|architect Guide

by Jonas Mariën

Zend Framework Web Services

Contents Copyright ©2010–2011 Jonas Mariën – All Rights Reserved
Book and cover layout, design and text Copyright ©2004-2011 Blue Parabola, LLC. and its predecessors – All Rights Reserved

First Edition: July 2011
ISBN: **978-0-98-103455-3**
Produced in Canada
Printed in the United States

No part of this book may be reproduced, stored in a retrieval system, or transmitted in any form or by means without the prior written permission of the publisher, except in the case of brief quotations embedded in critical reviews or articles.

Disclaimer

Although every effort has been made in the preparation of this book to ensure the accuracy of the information contained therein, this book is provided "as-is" and the publisher, the author(s), their distributors and retailers, as well as all affiliated, related or subsidiary parties take no responsibility for any inaccuracy and any and all damages caused, either directly or indirectly, by the use of such information. We have endeavoured to properly provide trademark information on all companies and products mentioned in the book by the appropriate use of capitals. However, we cannot guarantee the accuracy of such information.

Blue Parabola, The Blue Parabola logo, php|architect, the php|architect logo, NanoBook and the NanoBook logo are trademarks or registered trademarks of Blue Parabola, LLC, its assigns, partners, predecessors and successors.

Written by	Jonas Mariën
Published by	Blue Parabola, LLC.
	28 Bombay Ave.
	Toronto, ON M3H 1B7
	Canada
	(416) 630-6202 / (877) 630-6202
	info@phparch.com / www.phparch.com
Publisher	Marco Tabini
Technical Reviewer	Simon Harris
Copy Editor	Stan Tymorek and Lori Ann Pannier
Layout and Design	Arbi Arzoumani
Managing Editor	Elizabeth Tucker Long
Finance and Resource Management	Emanuela Corso

Contents

Chapter 1 — Zend Framework   3
   Introduction   3
   Why Zend Framework?   3
   Development Environment Setup   5
   Bootstrap the Project   8
   Summary 13

Chapter 2 — Our Data   17
   The Customer 17
      Their Case 17
   The Database Structure 18
   The Methods for the Web Service 20
   The Class Code 21
   Customer Requirements 24
   Summary 25

Chapter 3 — SOAP   27
   Introduction 27
   SOAP and PHP 28
      First Contact 28
      Plenty of Options 31
   Using Classes 32
   SoapParam, SoapVar and Classmaps 33
      SoapParam 33

CONTENTS

   SoapVar and Variable Types 34
   Persistence and Cookies 34
   Enter WSDL 35
   Classmaps 38
 Error Handling 40
 Debugging 42
 SOAP and Zend Framework 45
   Zend_Soap_Client 45
   Zend_Soap_Server 45
   Zend_Soap_Wsdl 47
   Zend_Soap_AutoDiscover 48
   Example Code 50
   Option 1: Separate Bootstrap Code in a Separate PHP File 51
   Option 2: Wrap it Inside a Controller 52
 Extending Zend_Soap 54
 Public and Private Web Services 57
   Logging, Versioning, Response and Error Codes 58
   Logging 58
   Versioning 58
   Error Codes 59
 Summary 60

Chapter 4 — Customizing Our SOAP Service 63

 Introduction 63
 Solution 1: Add an API Key Parameter to Each Method 63
   Pro and Cons 64
 Solution 2: Pre-parse the SOAP Message 65
   Pros and Cons 68
 Solution 3: Use Magic Methods 70
   Pros and Cons 72
 Summary 73

Chapter 5 — REST 75

 Introduction 75
 Some Background on REST 75

REST versus POX versus RPC versus Pure REST 79
    REST and PHP 80
Creating the REST Service Using Zend Framework 88
    Zend_Rest_Route 92
    Zend_Rest_Controller 94
Zend_Http_Client 95
    Some Example Code 97
Customize the REST Service 105
API Version in the URL 106
API Key and Preprocessing 109
Summary 112

Chapter 6 — XML-RPC — 115

Introduction 115
    system.listMethods 119
    system.methodSignature 120
    system.methodHelp 121
    system.multicall 121
    XML-RPC and PHP 122
    Creating the XML-RPC Service Using Zend Framework 126
    Zend_XmlRpc_Server 126
    Zend_XmlRpc_Client 127
More Zend_XmlRpc_Server 131
    Multiple Namespaces 131
    Encoding 131
    Faultcodes and Exceptions 131
    Caching 132
    XML Generation 133
    Customizing the XML-RPC Service 133
    API version in the URL 133
    API Key and Pre-processing 134
Summary 135

Chapter 7 — JSON-RPC　139

Introduction 139
Streams 140
HTTP 140
    Request 141
    Response 141
    Error Object 141
Batches 142
JSON-RPC and PHP 142
    Zend_Json_Server 143
    Zend_Json_Server_Smd 145
Connecting from JavaScript 147
What is Missing? 149
Customize the JSON-RPC Service 150
Summary 151

Chapter 8 — Limiting Access using Zend_Acl　153

Resources 153
Roles 154
Rules 155
Privileges 156
Where to Store the Rules 158
How to Use Zend_Acl in our Web Service Code 164
Add Checks to Existing Services 167
    SOAP 168
    REST 168
    XML-RPC 170
    JSON-RPC 171
Summary 172

Chapter 9 — Performance and Scaling　175

Introduction 175
Where to Search 175
    Network 175
    Server Hardware and Tiered Setup 176

Operating System 178
Web Server 178
Database 179
Code 180
How to Detect Bottlenecks 181
Monitoring Tools 181
Measurement and Benchmarks 182
Detecting Code Issues 183
Add Some Caching 184
Summary 187

Chapter 10 — Unit Testing   189

Introduction and Background 189
Enter PHPUnit 191
Test Fixtures 192
Test Cases and Test Suites 192
Execution 192
Assertions 193
Mocks and Stubs 194
Mocking Web Services Using PHPUnit 198
Testing the SOAP Service Setup and a Basic Call 198
Testing the REST Server Response 199
Summary 201

Chapter 11 — Security   205

Introduction and Background 205
Countermeasures 207
Use a Firewall 207
Use Additional Apache Modules 207
Check your Web Server 207
Check and Adapt Your Code 208
Securing Communication 208
One Step Further 209
Summary 210

Chapter 12 — End-User Documentation   **213**
   Introduction 213
   Summary 218

Chapter 13 — Conclusion   **221**

Chapter 14 — Appendices   **223**
   Appendix A: Development Environment Setup 223
      Links 223
      Linux 224
      Debian/Ubuntu 224
      Fedora 225
      CentOS 226
      Mac OS X 226
      Windows 226
      PHPUnit and Friends 227
      Memcached 227
   Appendix B: Specific Tools Used 228
      Apache mod_rewrite 228
      Stream Wrappers 229
      GET, POST, PUT, DELETE using cURL 230
      Sockets 231
   Appendix C: Potential Impact of ZF Moving to 2.0 231

Chapter 1

Zend Framework

Introduction

In this first chapter we will try to get up and running as fast as possible by showing how to set up and configure your web server, and how a basic Zend Framework application is constructed, which will stand us in good stead for the following chapters. This book is conceived as a hands-on guide, exploring actual code and technical details where possible, so if you are interested in tinkering and playing around with the code accompanying this book, you will need a working environment similar to the one described. If you already have some real life Zend Framework development experience, you will be able to skim over this chapter very quickly. If not, read it carefully and make sure you have everything working as it should before moving on.

Do not expect anything ground-breaking here. This book will get to real life examples as quickly as possible, and we'll keep this chapter short and clean.

Why Zend Framework?

Zend Framework is a PHP framework consisting of a growing collection of components. These components can be combined into a feature-complete MVC stack. Alternatively, many of them may be used separately or in conjunction with other frameworks and libraries.

Launched in 2006 by Zend Technologies, Inc - the company founded by the two original authors of the Zend Engine - Zend Framework quickly gained traction to become one of the better-known PHP frameworks. At the time of writing, it has been adopted by a large number of companies and considerable parts of the community.

Some consider Zend Framework, and frameworks in general, to be bloated and prefer their code custom-crafted for each task. Yet whenever development teams grow in size and customer demands grow even faster, the need for a clear application structure and code reusability becomes more urgent. This is where frameworks come into play, along with coding guidelines, unit testing, automatic API documentation and Continuous Integration systems. All of these techniques and their rise in popularity are part of a tendency in the PHP world towards more mature development practices, more mature teams and enterprise readiness.

Growing numbers of professional PHP developers use these techniques, taking their code to the next level using frameworks like Zend Framework, Symfony, Solar, Kohana, CakePHP and many, many others. Some of these frameworks are here to stay, while some will eventually disappear, and yet others will grow to an even more dominant position. Zend Framework, given its pedigree and the quality of the code, is most likely here to stay.

All good and well, but is this the only reason that Zend Framework is chosen for a book on web services? Not at all. Firstly, the components provided by the framework for web service creation are mature and well-designed. They offer good integration with the rest of the framework and are comprehensively documented. Secondly, the entire code is unit-tested and peer-reviewed. Thirdly, there is no licensing fuss around Zend Framework: the code is created from scratch and all contributors must sign an agreement which clearly regulates the licensing. Finally, I just like it. I had to pick one of the available frameworks for this book and Zend Framework seemed an obvious choice, at least to me.

For more information on Zend Framework, such as a detailed history and its positioning compared to other frameworks and solutions, there are plenty of online resources available. Many of these are centered around the Zend Framework website[1]. Among other things, you will find the Zend Framework reference manual there, as well as the option to file a bug report, and to browse the Subversion repositories and the development wiki.

---

[1] http://framework.zend.com

If you are a Zend Framework novice, going through the quick-start tutorial will be of great help and will introduce you to some key concepts in a very steady pace and comprehensive way.

Also, do note that a major new version of Zend Framework will be available in the coming months. On the website accompanying this book, the example code will be updated for this new version, along with some detailed notes where necessary. Appendix C has an overview of the potential impact of version 2.0 on our code.

Development Environment Setup

For your environment to be usable, you will need a web server and database server. I chose Apache and MySQL for this, since they are widely-used and well-known to most PHP developers. As for the operating system, I am an Ubuntu and Debian Linux user myself, but everything which follows should be possible on RPM-based distributions, on Windows, Mac OSX or even FreeBSD. Appendix A has some pointers on installing all the necessary tools on these other platforms.

Installation of Apache, PHP and accompanying services like MySQL can be done using `apt-get` on Debian systems and distributions derived from it:

```
apt-get install apache2 libapache2-mod-php5 php5 php5-common php5-cli php5-mysql
    php5-xmlrpc  mysql-client-5.1 mysql-common mysql-server
```

If you are prompted for input on some configuration choices, just accept the defaults, as they should be sufficient for now. You should also enable the Apache `mod_rewrite` module, using the command `a2enmod rewrite`.

Throughout this book the latest version of Zend Framework available at the time of writing will be used, which is currently version 1.10.2. Zend provides a choice of the full or minimal versions, with the latter containing only the library's standard components, and this version will serve us well. Download the framework from the Zend Framework website[2] and unpack:

```
mkdir -p /web/zfws/ && cd /web/zfws
```

---

[2] http://framework.zend.com

6 ■ Zend Framework

```
wget http://framework.zend.com/releases/ZendFramework-1.10.2/ZendFramework
    -1.10.2-minimal.tar.gz
tar zxvf ZendFramework-1.10.2-minimal.tar.gz
mv ZendFramework-1.10.2-minimal/library .
mv ZendFramework-1.10.2-minimal/bin .
rm -rf ZendFramework-1.10.2-minimal
```

The `library/` directory contains all of the Zend Framework components. The `bin/` directory contains the Zend_Tool scripts for bootstrapping our project code.

Now, for ease of use, you could let the user and group running Apache own the entire source tree. On Debian Linux, you could do something like this:

```
chown -R www-data.www-data /web/zfws
chmod -R g+w /web/zfws
```

This makes the tree writable for the `www-data` group. You can add your own user to the `www-data` group by adding `www-data` to your group memberships. Replace "jonas" with your own username in the following command:

```
usermod -a -G www-data jonas
```

Do note that the above is not considered good practice for a production environment, since an Apache user should not be able to write files all over the place. More on this and security in general can be found in Chapter 11.

Now let's define a virtual host for Apache, so that our web server knows where to find the files for our site. The contents of the file you should create in `/etc/apache2/sites-available/zfws` are as follows:

```
<VirtualHost *:80>
    ServerAdmin you@example.com
    ServerName zfws
    DocumentRoot /web/zfws/public
    <Directory />
      AllowOverride None
    </Directory>
    <Directory /web/zfws/public>
      Options Indexes FollowSymLinks MultiViews
      AllowOverride All
      Order allow,deny
```

```
        allow from all
    </Directory>
    setenv APPLICATION_ENV development
    LogLevel warn
    ErrorLog /var/log/apache2/zfws-error.log
    CustomLog /var/log/apache2/zfws-access.log combined
</VirtualHost>
```

Now enable the virtual host by running `a2ensite zfws` as root, and restart the Apache process by running `/etc/init.d/apache2 reload`. The only thing left to do to make the site respond to requests from our local development environment is point the "zfws" hostname to the `127.0.0.1` loopback address. Simply add this to the end of the `/etc/hosts` file:

```
127.0.0.1 zfws
```

Since nothing resides under the `public/` directory yet, there is nothing to see in a browser, but we will soon change that. Also note that no library or application code will be placed inside our public directory, rather it will be placed outside our document root.

In Chapter 2, our database, which will contain the data to be exposed through our web services, will be created. You can install MySQL 5+ using your package manager, as we did when we executed the installation commands above, or use an install package from the MySQL website[3]. A MySQL management tool such as MySQL Administrator (check under *GUI Tools* at the MySQL site) or good old phpMyAdmin can help you to manage your database. MySQL also has a number of command-line tools such as `mysql` and `mysqladmin` which allow you to manage your database using low-level yet powerful commands. We use the Ubuntu supplied MySQL 5.1 version, but the code was also tested on MySQL 5.0. You can check for your installed version by running this query:

```
SELECT VERSION();
```

---

[3] http://www.mysql.com

Finally, you need a decent code editor or Integrated Development Environment (IDE). Numerous alternatives are available these days, from the free Netbeans and Eclipse PDT packages to paid-for software such as PHPEd, Komodo IDE, Zend Studio and phpStorm. Just pick one you like and feel comfortable working in. A good IDE is a real asset and speeds up your development cycle. Remember to use UTF-8 file encoding for all your PHP files to avoid for character encoding issues later on.

Bootstrap the Project

Zend_Tool provides several useful scripts to help get a project started. This command will create most of the application directory layout:

```
cd /web/zfws
./bin/zf.sh create project .
```

That command uses the `zf.sh` command-line tool, which in turn uses Zend_Tool to generate the necessary directories containing basic Zend_Application-based MVC code. The inner workings of Zend_Tool are beyond the scope of this work, and the online Zend Framework reference manual has in-depth information on the tool and its use. There is a Windows variant of the command line tool called `zf.bat`.

The three directories Zend_Tool created that are of most interest to us right now, are as follows:

- **application:** our application-specific code will be found here
- **library:** this contains the `Zend/` directory which holds all Zend Framework components
- **public:** contains `index.php`, the default index file which will load the necessary libraries from `library/` and runs Zend_Application, which in turn will load everything it needs from `application/`.

Inside `application` you will find several more directories and a file named `Bootstrap.php`. An overview of the folder layout is shown in the following example:

```
application
    |-- Bootstrap.php
    |-- configs
    |     '-- application.ini
    |-- controllers
    |     |-- ErrorController.php
    |     '-- IndexController.php
    |-- models
    '-- views
        |-- helpers
        '-- scripts
            |-- error
            |    '-- error.phtml
            '-- index
                '-- index.phtml
library
public
 |-- .htaccess
 '-- index.php
tests
```

The main application configuration file `application.ini` will look similar to the following:

```
[production]
phpSettings.display_startup_errors = 0
phpSettings.display_errors = 0
includePaths.library = APPLICATION_PATH "/../library"
bootstrap.path = APPLICATION_PATH "/Bootstrap.php"
bootstrap.class = "Bootstrap"
appnamespace = "Application"
resources.frontController.controllerDirectory = APPLICATION_PATH "/controllers"
resources.frontController.params.displayExceptions = 0

[staging : production]

[testing : production]
phpSettings.display_startup_errors = 1
phpSettings.display_errors = 1

[development : production]
phpSettings.display_startup_errors = 1
phpSettings.display_errors = 1
resources.frontController.params.displayExceptions = 1
```

This contains basic information for Zend_Application setup and configuration information for reusable **resources**, such as database connections, which will - more or less automagically - be made available to the application. `Bootstrap.php` is also part of the Zend_Application bootstrap flow and allows for the creation of additional resources which are not out-of-the-box supported as Zend_Application resources. You can also manipulate resources described in `application.ini` inside this class.

A common example of a resource which can be defined in `application.ini` is a database connection, since a resource definition for it is provided for you by the framework, in `library/Zend/Application/Resource/Db.php`. On the other hand, a caching layer using Zend_Cache would be an example of a resource you would create and configure manually inside a class method in `Bootstrap.php`. That method would be named something along the lines of `_initCache()`, as any methods whose names begin with the prefix "_init" and are defined within the `Bootstrap` class will be run automatically by the bootstrap procedure.

Remember also that `application.ini` is parsed by Zend_Config, and as such supports sections and inheritance between sections. There are sections for "production" and "development", and development inherits most settings from "production". In our virtual host configuration file above, we used the `SetEnv` directive to define an environment variable with the name `APPLICATION_ENV` and the value "development". This results in Zend_Application parsing the "development" section of `application.ini`. This also makes it possible to define different database connections for production and development purposes and allow for more explicit error display during development.

The `application/controllers/` directory contains two controllers: the default index controller in `IndexController.php`, and an error controller in `ErrorController.php`. The index controller contains the action method `indexAction()`, while the error controller contains `errorAction()`. If you have Apache's mod_rewrite module enabled, URLs for your application are mapped (thanks to some rules inside `.htaccess`) as follows: `http://zfws/index/index`, `http://zfws/index` and `http://zfws/` all map to the index action of the index controller.

Suppose there is an action method named `detailAction()` in the `IndexController`, then `http://zfws/index/detail` and `http://zfws/detail` would both map to that action. Errors like application errors (if for example an exception in the code has been caught by the MVC stack) are routed to the `errorAction()` method of the `ErrorController`.

Do note that once you start working using **modules** (a separate directory containing views, controllers and models relating to a subset of the application's functionality), the controllers, views and models directly under the application folder are considered to be part of the *default* module. Creating a module is as simple as running the commands:

```
cd /web/zfws
./bin/zf.sh create module admin
./bin/zf.sh create controller index index-action-included=1 admin
```

This will create a modules directory containing controllers and an index view script. You can enable modules support in `application.ini`, by adding the following lines:

```
resources.frontController.moduleDirectory = APPLICATION_PATH "/modules"
resources.modules[] = "admin"
```

Now check the URLs `http://zfws/admin/index` and `http://zfws/admin/index/index`. They should map to the index action in the index controller in `modules/admin/controllers/IndexController.php`.

Zend Framework allows for heavy modification of the **routes** in your application to make your URLs even more user friendly, or to define aliases when things are moved around, for example during refactoring.

Typically **views** are called from a controller action and bear a similar name. If you point your browser to `http://zfws` you will see the resulting default Zend Framework welcome page (see Figure 1.1). The index action inside `IndexController.php` will be fired and the corresponding view in `views/scripts/index/index.phtml` will be parsed and displayed as the resulting default page. Views are written in PHP. Combining Zend Framework with a templating engine is quite possible but in general the built-in view mechanism should give you plenty of flexibility.

Models, the last directory left unmentioned until now will contain model classes, giving you an object-oriented way of retrieving and manipulating your data. The use of models in Zend Framework has led to heated debates in the past. Some want them to be lightweight and without much business logic inside, others place almost

12 ■ Zend Framework

Figure 1.1

the entire logic found in the application inside these models and make the V and C parts of the MVC of less importance.

For the code being built throughout this book, we will make use of fairly simple models, most of the time based on Zend_Db_Table, a Table Data Gateway[4] implementation which will provide a very convenient way of working with the data in our database tables. The models more or less represent the corresponding tables one-to-one. Calls like `$model->find(10)` will return an object of class `Zend_Db_Table_Row` representing the row from the table where the primary key equals "10". We will see more on this in the next few chapters, whenever we deal with the data in the MySQL database.

Now you might ask yourself: why do we need all this MVC code with views, routing, controllers and resources being bootstrapped if we are just going to build some web services? For some cases, this is indeed unnecessary. A SOAP service could be run from a procedural script which launches a `SoapServer` with only a few lines of code, but on the other hand, both SOAP and REST services can be integrated well with the Zend_Application MVC approach. The overhead of launching a SOAP service from the MVC stack and how to avoid it eventually will be covered further in Chapter 3, and we'll look at performance in general in more depth in Chapter 9. For now, we will take baby steps to arrive at multiple types of web services combined with a simple Zend Framework application setup.

Don't forget to double-check file ownerships and permissions on the freshly-generated application files. You need write access to be able to change them so run the `chown` and `chmod` commands again if you need to.

Summary

You should now have:

- a fresh development environment with a basic website inside its own virtual host

- all the Zend Framework files and application bootstrap code in place for our next steps

---

[4] http://www.martinfowler.com/eaaCatalog/tableDataGateway.html

- MySQL ready and waiting for the database which we are to import

So, let's move forward to the next chapter, where we'll populate our database in preparation for building web services on top of it.

Chapter 2

Our Data

The Customer

All example code in this book is based on a project for a fictitious client, "Marble Toys & Associates" who we'll refer to throughout the text as "MTA". This company produces toys and wants to open its warehouse and ordering system to third parties. Their back end system is entirely written in some obscure language, and they want to go for a quick win and open it using web services connecting directly to the underlying MySQL database. This example scenario provides context for the code and web services explained in the next chapters.

Their Case

MTA has multiple sales channels: online web shops run by partners, retail stores and chains and finally a web shop where MTA sells toys under a separate brand name.

Partner websites want to be able to check approximate stock figures, place back orders and fetch images of the products. The retail stores are part of a larger chain that asks for an API to automate orders and query stock numbers. Finally, the MTA web shop is non-maintainable and is going to be replaced by a front end that will use the API to fetch and display images, retrieve invoices and calculate shipping costs.

All of the mentioned sales channels need their own set of public methods for communicating. MTA wants to use API keys to limit access per client for parts of the web service and allow for flexibility in changing this access later on, when deemed necessary. When creating our web service, we will need to take this into account as well.

The Database Structure

We have a few tables in the database, relating to products on one hand, and orders on the other. Diagrams depicting the relationships visually can be seen in Figure 2.1 and Figure 2.2.

Products are organized into categories and can optionally be labeled using tags. A stock table refers to the product ID and holds stock information as accounted for in the warehouse. These tables could no doubt be normalized further or structured differently, but the tables proposed are purely for the sake of the example.

The tables organizing orders and invoices are also depicted. An order refers to an invoice which could group multiple orders, and also to products. The relationship to the products table is not shown here, so the overall image can be split into smaller parts for display. An invoice refers to a customer and an optional shipping ID. Individual orders can have different customer IDs from the ones used in the invoice, which is why the orders table also refers to the customers table.

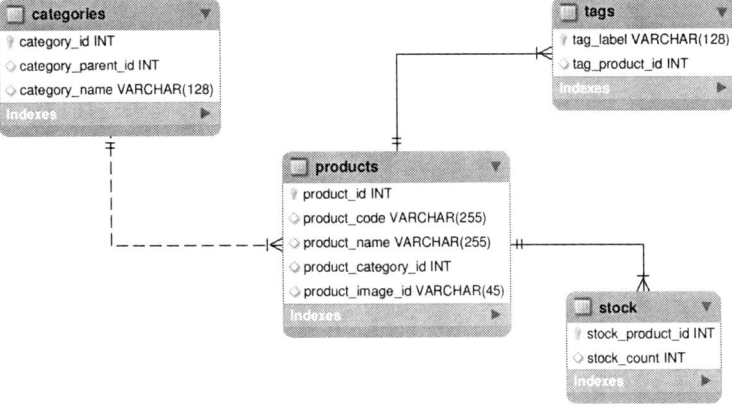

Figure 2.1

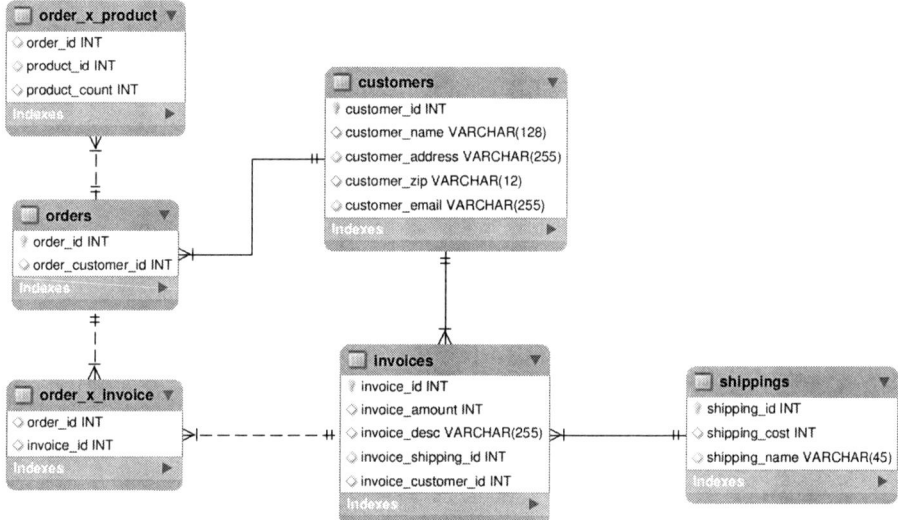

Figure 2.2

All code for creating the tables is included in the sample code accompanying this book, inside the sql/ directory. There are three files that will allow you to create the database and its tables and enter some sample data.

The statements in zfws-createdb-and-user.sql will result in a new database **zfws** and a new user **zfws** with sufficient privileges on this database. The password set for the zfws user is **zfws**. This should of course be changed into something more secure.

```
mysql -u root -p < zfws-createdb-and-user.sql
```

You will need to use the -p option if the root user has a password set, as it should. All of the necessary tables should be created by running:

```
mysql -u zfws -p zfws < zfws-create-tables.sql
```

Now you should enter **zfws** as the password, since you are running the queries in zfws-create-tables.sql as the zfws user.

Some sample data will be added by running this next command:

```
mysql -u zfws -p zfws < zfws-sample-data.sql
```

Again, you should enter the password for the zfws user here. In case you need to empty your tables, we also provided a file `zfws-delete-data.sql`. The TRUNCATE statements in this file will empty the tables in the correct order, taking into account the dependencies between the tables.

The Methods for the Web Service

Our requirements so far include those of the online store run by partners, who wish to be able to:

- check approximate stock figures
- place back orders
- fetch images for products

Retail stores and chains want to:

- have all of the above
- place, update and remove orders
- check order status

Finally, the MTA web shop requires:

- all of the above
- the ability to retrieve invoices
- a method for calculating order shipping costs

This means that in an ideal world we have a collection of methods that will be made available selectively to all partners. That should allow us to build on a single codebase and minimize development overhead for ourselves.

To be entirely clear, we are not going to build each and every part as stated in the requirements throughout this book. What we will produce as sample code however should be sufficient to help you create something adequate for the job.

The Class Code

We are going to create our own library named "Mta_Service" under the library/ directory and name it after the customer, MTA. Following Zend Framework's naming conventions, that will result in a directory named library/Mta/.

To enable Zend_Application to autoload the correct classes from the correct location, add this to the application.ini file:

```
autoloaderNamespaces.mta = "Mta_"
```

The following code should give you an idea of the available methods and method names we have in mind for the web service we're going to create:

```
class Mta_Service
{

  /**
   * @param    int $customer_id   customer identifier
   * @return   array|object
   */
  public function getCatalogue($customer_id, $category = '*')
  {
      Zend_Loader::loadFile(APPLICATION_PATH . '/models/Product.php');
      $catalogue = new Mta_Model_Product();
      return $catalogue->getItems($customer_id, $category);
  }


  /**
   * @param    int $product_id    product identifier
   * @return   int                 quantity available
   */
```

```php
public function getStockFigures($product_id)
{
    Zend_Loader::loadFile(APPLICATION_PATH . '/models/Stock.php');
    $stock = new Mta_Model_Stock();
    return $stock->getAvailable($product_id);
}


/**
 * @param    int $product_id    product identifier
 * @param    int $quantity
 * @return   int   backorder id
 */
public function createBackOrder($product_id, $quantity)
{
    Zend_Loader::loadFile(APPLICATION_PATH . '/models/Order.php');
    $order = new Mta_Model_Order();
    return $order->backOrder($product_id, $quantity);
}


/**
 * @param    int $product_id    product identifier
 * @return   string   image URL
 */
public function getImageLocation($product_id)
{
    Zend_Loader::loadFile(APPLICATION_PATH . '/models/Product.php');
    $product = new Mta_Model_Product();
    return $product->getImage($product_id);
}


/**
 * @param    int $product_id    product identifier
 * @param    int $customer_id   customer identifier
 * @return   int  order id for the newly created order
 */
public function createOrder($product_id, $customer_id)
{
    Zend_Loader::loadFile(APPLICATION_PATH . '/models/Order.php');
    $order = new Mta_Model_Order();
    return $order->create($product_id, $customer_id, $cnt);
}
```

```
/**
 * @param   int $order_id    order identifier
 * @return  string  message containing a code
 */
public function getOrderStatus($order_id)
{
    Zend_Loader::loadFile(APPLICATION_PATH . '/models/Order.php');
    $order = new Mta_Model_Order();
    return $order->getStatus($order_id);
}

//... and so on ...

}
```

There are many more methods that we can imagine, but the above is sufficient to serve as an example. Our class code will also be tweaked whenever the need arises. The objects `Mta_Model_Order`, `Mta_Model_Stock` and `Mta_Model_Product` used inside the code are created using Zend_Db_Table-based models, all of them holding some business logic related to the underlying tables. In a more mature application, this would probably evolve toward the use of an Object-Relational Mapper such as Doctrine.

An example class for accessing the table containing invoice information may look like this, if based on Zend_Db_Table.

```
<?php
class Mta_Model_Invoice extends Zend_Db_Table_Abstract
{
    protected $_name = 'invoices';
}
```

Adding this next method to the application `Bootstrap` class will allow the entire application, even from a module, to load the model from the common models directory:

```
protected function _initAppAutoload()
{
    $autoloader = new Zend_Application_Module_Autoloader(array(
        'namespace' => 'Mta',
        'basePath'  => APPLICATION_PATH,
    ));
```

```
    return $autoloader;
}
```

The database layer we use is thin, but remember we're talking about web services, not about application design *per se*. We want the examples to have a somewhat realistic feel, but some compromise is necessary to make sure we do not digress too far from the main points.

Don't forget that to be able to actually use the database, you can add a resource to the application.ini file, just like this:

```
;db connection resource
resources.db.adapter = PDO_MYSQL
resources.db.params.host = localhost
resources.db.params.port = 3306
resources.db.params.username = zfws
resources.db.params.password = zfws
resources.db.params.dbname = zfws
resources.db.profiler.enabled = false
resources.db.isDefaultTableAdapter = true
```

Resources are made available automatically by using Zend_Application, which is exactly what we are going to do in our bootstrap code further on.

Customer Requirements

Time for some requirements gathering: let's summarize what we have so far:

- The customers want a web service or API to open up parts of their internal ordering and product database.

- They want support for REST and RPC style techniques.

- It should be possible to reuse the same code and open/close parts of the service depending on the client using the web service. They prefer the use of an API key to identify the client.

Some additional requirements are provided by their IT department:

- They want the service to scale well in case it is successful. We should keep that in mind when building our solution.

- End-user documentation should be easy to create and update on-the-fly if possible.

- Some automated testing, eventually based on unit testing.

- The web service has to be secure.

Nothing much, nor very detailed, but it is a starting point. Most of us have started coding with even less information!

Remember, throughout the rest of the book it will be mentioned whenever we have something ready that meets one or more of the requirements. We will not conclude with a fully functional solution in the example code accompanying this book, but by reading the next chapters and with some tinkering you could easily have something ready that meets these requirements.

Summary

In this chapter we briefly touched on matters unrelated to web services. This was necessary to build more meaningful examples in the next chapters. Some of you realized that *actual* methods are going to be exposed *just like that*. Others are shrugging and want to get their hands dirty. This is exactly what we will do in Chapter 3, which covers building web services using SOAP.

Chapter 3

SOAP

Introduction

Simple Object Access Protocol, more commonly known as SOAP, is a web service protocol that uses XML as its underlying message format. The World Wide Web Consortium (W3C) has recognized SOAP as a standard since version 1.2, which was released in 2003. It was conceived with Microsoft as one of its main supporters and this simple fact alone appears to be a reason for some to regard it with some suspicion. In my opinion, there is no reason to do so.

SOAP is method oriented, so in its simplest form, you can think of a SOAP request as a call to a function, more correctly known as an operation, which is executed on a remote server: the SOAP server. A function call has parameters and thus, some knowledge about the method signature is required.

There are two versions of SOAP in the wild: SOAP 1.1 and SOAP 1.2, and the SOAP website[1] has a rundown of the differences between the two). A brief summary follows:

- SOAP 1.2 allows for transport of the messages over means other than HTTP, making SOAP network protocol agnostic

---
[1] http://www.w3.org/2003/06/soap11-soap12.html

- Since SOAP 1.2, the acronym itself is no longer considered a short notation for Simple Object Access Protocol
- If you have a choice, use SOAP 1.2, as it has been around since 2003 and, perhaps more importantly, is governed by a W3C working group

SOAP and PHP

PHP has had good built-in SOAP support since PHP5, and the protocol has become popular in the PHP community over the past few years. One reason for its popularity is that you can have your own PHP-based SOAP server up and running with only a few lines of code.

The SOAP extension is enabled by default in recent PHP builds for most operating systems. If it is not available for your platform, you might consider switching platforms or building it yourself, by compiling PHP using the -enable-soap configuration option. The SOAP extension has some runtime flags which can be set in the php.ini file or directly in your code. An important feature, for example, is the ability to turn on or off the caching of web service description (WSDL) files, which you should turn off while developing (look for soap.wsdl_cache_enabled in the PHP manual).

Be aware that PHP uses SOAP 1.1 by default. You can avoid this by explicitly specifying the required SOAP version when instantiating the client or server. Code examples further on will show how to achieve this.

First Contact

Here is an example. The following code can be saved as soapserver.php on your local web server and effectively creates a SOAP server with a method someMathConstant(). This method expects a single argument, the type of mathematic constant we want in order to get the value for:

```php
<?php

function someMathConstant($constant)
{
   switch($constant) {
      case 'pi':
```

```
            return '3.14159265';
            break;
        case 'e':
            return 'be rational';
            break;
        default:
            return 'unknown variable';
            break;
    }
}

$server = new SoapServer(null, array('uri' => 'http://zfws/', 'soap_version' =>
    SOAP_1_2));
$server->addFunction("someMathConstant");
$server->handle();
```

As you can see for yourself, creating a basic SOAP server in PHP is easy. In our example we use the `SoapServer` class provided by PHP's SOAP extension, and explicitly tell it to use SOAP 1.2. The exact same argument can be passed to the `SoapClient` class too. Also note that you can export multiple functions at once, by passing an array of function names as the argument for `addFunction()`. You could even pass the constant `SOAP_FUNCTIONS_ALL` as the only argument, which will allow every PHP function to be exposed through your SOAP server: but of course this would also put your entire server at high risk.

Alternatively, you can catch the input and hand it over to the SOAP server instead of letting it handle the incoming request:

```
$server = new SoapServer(...);
...
$data = file_get_contents('php://input');
$server->handle($data);
```

If you point your browser at that `soapserver.php` file, let's say at `http://zfws/soapserver.php`, you will end up with an empty page. It expects an HTTP POST request containing structured data in XML format. The server is there but simply hasn't received a request it is able to handle. We can create a SOAP call using PHP for testing our new server however. Here is `soapclient.php`, which creates an example `SoapClient` object for interfacing with our SOAP server:

30 ■ SOAP

```php
<?php

try {
    $client = new SoapClient(null,
        array(
            'location'     => "http://zfws/soapserver.php",
            'uri'          => "http://zfws/",
            'soap_version' => SOAP_1_2
        )
    );

    echo $client->someMathConstant('pi');
} catch (Exception $e) {
    echo $e->getMessage();
}
```

The "uri" option in the second parameter (an options array) refers to the SOAP server namespace, while the "location" option refers to the actual location of the web service.

Executing `soapclient.php` results in the number PI being displayed on your screen. So, creating a SOAP client is as easy as creating a server.

Now let's take a look at the actual messages sent over the wire. The request looks like this:

```xml
<soapenv:Envelope XMLns:xsi="http://www.w3.org/2001/XMLSchema-instance" XMLns:
    xsd="http://www.w3.org/2001/XMLSchema" XMLns:soapenv="http://schemas.XMLsoap
    .org/soap/envelope/" XMLns:som="somemath">
  <soapenv:Header/>
  <soapenv:Body>
    <som:someMathConstant soapenv:encodingStyle="http://schemas.XMLsoap.org/
        soap/encoding/">
      <Request xsi:type="xsd:string">pi</Request>
    </som:someMathConstant>
  </soapenv:Body>
</soapenv:Envelope>
```

And the response:

```xml
<SOAP-ENV:Envelope SOAP-ENV:encodingStyle="http://schemas.XMLsoap.org/soap/
    encoding/" XMLns:SOAP-ENV="http://schemas.XMLsoap.org/soap/envelope/" XMLns:
    ns1="somemath" XMLns:xsd="http://www.w3.org/2001/XMLSchema" XMLns:xsi="http
```

```
    ://www.w3.org/2001/XMLSchema-instance" XMLns:SOAP-ENC="http://schemas.
    XMLsoap.org/soap/encoding/">
  <SOAP-ENV:Body>
    <ns1:someMathConstantResponse>
       <Result xsi:type="xsd:string">3.14159265</Result>
    </ns1:someMathConstantResponse>
  </SOAP-ENV:Body>
</SOAP-ENV:Envelope>
```

The root XML tag `Envelope` in the `SOAP-ENV` namespace is the SOAP envelope, and usually consists of a header and a body. This is a lot of XML for just a few pieces of actual data, causing many supporters of other protocols and techniques, such as REST, to think SOAP is bloated and has too much overhead. When you have a simple example like the one we're working with, some of this criticism is probably correct. However, when matters become more complex, as they tend to do in real-life scenarios, the data-versus-overhead ratio starts to improve quickly.

Plenty of Options

You should also be aware that even if instantiating a SOAP client looks simple, PHP's SOAP support is quite powerful. Consider the following example:

```
<?php
$client = new SoapClient(null, array('location'  => "https://example.com/soap.
    php",
                                     'uri'        => "https://example.com/"
                                     'local_cert' => "clientcert.pem",
                                     'passphrase' => "passphrase"));
```

Here you pass an optional client-side certificate upon client instantiation. This is just one of the many optional parameters that you can explore for your needs.

You can also add extra headers to the SOAP envelope itself by using the `SoapHeader` class. Here we add extra headers allowing us to authenticate before accessing the web service. If the remote SOAP server has a `createSomething()` method but expects some authentication through SOAP headers first, we can use the lower level `__soapCall()` method to execute our call.

This method accepts the remote operation name, parameters for that operation and the optional headers we created, and calls the web service using all of the information we gave it. This allows for adding the extra, required headers.

```
$credentials = new StdClass();
$credentials->user = 'yourusername';
$credentials->pass = 'yourpass';
$extraheaders = new SoapVar($credentials, SOAP_ENC_OBJECT);
$header = new SoapHeader("http://example.com/", "Authenticate", $extraheaders);
$client->__soapCall("createSomething", array($product_id, $quantity), null,
    $header);
```

As an alternative to using `__soapCall()`, you can create the same `SoapVar` encoded object containing credentials and set them explicitly as headers before calling the remote method:

```
$client->__setSoapHeaders(array($header));
$client->createSomething();
```

We will discuss `SoapVar` again later on in this chapter.

Other examples of settings and properties that you can modify by explicitly defining them through the SOAP headers include parameters for setting compression levels for the HTTP transport and additional proxy-server settings to use when connecting to the remote web service.

So, plenty of configuration options exist, and tweaking is possible when consuming a remote web service.

Using Classes

What if the code we want to expose grows more complex? All of the previous code simply added a single function to the web service to be exposed. You will hardly ever do that once you start creating SOAP web services on the job. Adding a class and exposing the public methods contained inside is a much more convenient strategy for launching a SOAP server:

```
<?php
```

```
class someMath
{
   public function someMathConstant($constant)
   {
      // ...
   }
}

$server = new SoapServer(null, array('uri' => 'http://zfws/','soap_version' =>
    SOAP_1_2));
$server->setClass('someMath');
$server->handle();
```

Now you have a web service that exposes any methods that are declared public. One of the main advantages is the ability to quickly reuse existing classes to be exposed. Overall this is a much more flexible way of launching our SOAP service.

Finally, there exists a third and perhaps even more interesting way to add existing methods to a SOAP server: `SoapServer::setObject()`. This allows for adding an object rather than a class as the supplier of the SOAP server's methods. Combined with standard object-oriented techniques such as composition, this can result in a great deal of additional flexibility when launching a service based on existing code.

SoapParam, SoapVar and Classmaps

Some concepts were left unmentioned or were covered only briefly in the previous paragraphs, for the sake of simplicity. We shall now discuss some of those concepts in more depth.

SoapParam

The `SoapParam` class allows for the correct passing of parameters to the remote operations. In the wonderful world of WSDL, which we'll cover shortly, you won't need to explicitly encode parameters and variables yourself, as this is handled for you. If you have no choice, however, you can wrap your methods call's parameters in a `SoapParam` object, which will spare you a few headaches:

```php
<?php
$client = new SoapClient(null,array('location' => "http://example.com/soap.php",
                                    'uri'      => "http://example.com/"));
$client->someFunction(new SoapParam($a, "a"), new SoapParam($b, "b"));
```

Here we pass $a and tell the remote method that $a is actually the expected parameter "a." You can explicitly set all required parameters like this, which should result in clearly defined requests and expected responses.

SoapVar and Variable Types

SoapVar is another SOAP helper class built into PHP, and is used for properly encoding variables to their corresponding SOAP message artifacts. A typical SoapVar object is created like this:

```
$soapstruct = new SoapVar($object, SOAP_ENC_OBJECT);
```

In addition to SOAP_ENC_OBJECT and SOAP_ENC_ARRAY there are other defined constants referring to SOAP types; like XSD_STRING and XSD_BOOLEAN. SoapVar accepts more parameters such as the type name, which is defined in an XML Schema Definition (XSD) file, and the path to that XSD file. This allows the mapping of PHP types such as "string" and "boolean" to their SOAP counterparts. Defining more complex types such as a PHP array or object can be done using XSD definitions. When we discuss WSDL further, this will be explained in greater detail.

Persistence and Cookies

You can maintain a session between subsequent requests by telling the SOAP server explicitly how to handle persistence. The public setPersistence() method accepts one of these predefined constants:

- SOAP_PERSISTENCE_REQUEST: results in the object being persisted during the request, much as you might expect

- SOAP_PERSISTENCE_SESSION: passing this as the argument will result in the object being persisted for the duration of a session

This will only work if the methods being exported by the SOAP server were added using a class or object.

A SOAP client can use the `__setCookie()` method to define a cookie name and value as parameters. This cookie will be sent along with the request. Sending this cookie in all following requests allows the server to recognize the session by checking `$_COOKIE['cookiename']` against an existing session, and therefore to restore the state.

All in all, it's good to know that you can tell a client to send a cookie with the request, as some remote SOAP servers may require it. However, I would not rely on it when creating a SOAP expected service yourself: it is not well documented, it does not handle custom session handlers and there are other means of identifying the user who issues subsequent requests against your expected service. Requiring an API key to be passed into every call is a common practice, for example.

Enter WSDL

So far so good: we're able to expose locally defined functions as SOAP service methods. Let's beef this up a little. Enter WSDL, the web Service Description Language, often pronounced "wiz-del" or "whiz-dull". Like SOAP, it is based on XML and allows for describing a web service, complete with its methods and the input and output messages expected by these methods. Just like SOAP 1.2, it is adopted as a recommendation by the W3C as of version 2.0. Through WSDL, more complex data types can be described and enforced by clients consuming the web service. Like SOAP envelopes, WSDL files can become quite verbose; and creating a WSDL file by hand is not always an easy task.

Many of the more advanced IDEs can use a WSDL file for code hinting of remote method names and their parameters when you point a `SoapClient` object towards that WSDL file. This can be very helpful indeed. Even better, some IDEs can analyze existing code, for example a class to be exposed via `SoapServer`, and create a WSDL file for it.

Creating a WSDL file by hand is not always a pleasant task, and some editors like Zend Studio even allow you to "automagically" generate a WSDL file based on existing code. The earlier versions of Zend Studio did so as do the newer, Eclipse-based ones.

There are even some libraries and pieces of code available on the web that can inspect your code and create an example WSDL file for you, too. While for a long time NuSOAP was the only decent library available for performing more advanced SOAP and WSDL handling, nowadays there are multiple solutions.

The more advanced tools use reflection, along with your own comments inside the docblocks that accompany your methods. Be aware however that creating a WSDL file using these tools may require some manual tweaking: Unless, of course, you use a mature library like Zend Framework's SOAP component. This provides you with end-to-end tools to create a SOAP server and corresponding WSDL file with a great deal of ease.

What follows is an example WSDL file for our code, which was initially generated using Zend Studio and then modified by hand to actually work with our example:

```xml
<?xml version ='1.0' encoding ='UTF-8' ?>
<definitions name='somemath'
  targetNamespace='http://zfws/somemath'
  xmlns:tns='http://zfws/somemath'
  xmlns:soap='http://schemas.xmlsoap.org/wsdl/soap/'
  xmlns:xsd='http://www.w3.org/2001/XMLSchema'
  xmlns:soapenc='http://schemas.xmlsoap.org/soap/encoding/'
  xmlns:wsdl='http://schemas.xmlsoap.org/wsdl/'
  xmlns='http://schemas.xmlsoap.org/wsdl/'>
<message name='someMathConstantRequest'>
  <part name='Request' type='xsd:string'/>
</message>
<message name='someMathConstantResponse'>
  <part name='Result' type='xsd:string'/>
</message>
<portType name='someMathConstantPortType'>
  <operation name='someMathConstant'>
    <input message='tns:someMathConstantRequest'/>
    <output message='tns:someMathConstantResponse'/>
  </operation>
</portType>
<binding name='someMathConstantBinding' type='tns:someMathConstantPortType'>
  <soap:binding style='rpc'
    transport='http://schemas.xmlsoap.org/soap/http'/>
  <operation name='someMathConstant'>
    <soap:operation soapAction='urn:somemath'/>
    <input>
      <soap:body use='encoded' namespace='somemath'
        encodingStyle='http://schemas.xmlsoap.org/soap/encoding/'/>
```

```
      </input>
      <output>
        <soap:body use='encoded' namespace='somemath'
          encodingStyle='http://schemas.xmlsoap.org/soap/encoding/'/>
      </output>
    </operation>
  </binding>
  <service name='someMathConstantService'>
    <port name='someMathConstantPort' binding='tns:someMathConstantBinding'>
      <soap:address location='http://zfws/soapserver.php'/>
    </port>
  </service>
</definitions>
```

As previously mentioned, this code is quite verbose, when you consider that the only thing it actually does is describe a method, its input parameter(s) and return value type. Let's have a closer look at what we have:

- `portType`: this describes the service operations (methods like `someMathConstant()` in our example) and input and output messages involved in these operations

- `message`: describes the parameters being sent to the operations and the responses returned

- `binding`: this ties the operation to a certain location or "port"

- `service`: a formal description of the service, usually pointing to a URL

One thing missing in our example is a "types" section. Here specific or additional types besides the standard ones like `xsd:string` can be defined in XML Schema.

By the way, the `xsd:` namespace is defined on the W3 website[2] and `soap-enc:` on the XMLsoap.org website[3]. The target namespace for a service is typically defined as `tns:` and is usually specific to the web service at hand.

The code we wrote to allow launching our SOAP server can now be simplified to look like this:

---

[2] http://www.w3.org/2001/XMLSchema
[3] http://schemas.XMLsoap.org/soap/encoding

```
$server = new SoapServer("somemath.wsdl");
```

And our client code is much simpler too:

```
$client = new SoapClient("http://zfws/somemath.wsdl");
```

We no longer need the second argument to define a range of options for the constructor if we have a WSDL file, since we are now working in WSDL mode. We don't have to use `SoapVar` and `SoapParam` since the information provided by them is now mainly contained within the WSDL file. Again, you don't *need* a WSDL file, as you can create and use SOAP services without it, but it makes the development of SOAP clients and servers so much easier, as you can see.

If you are interested in reading further about WSDL, there is plenty of information available online, and don't forget to have a look at Universal Description, Discovery and Integration (UDDI). This directory service allows for easy publishing and exploration of WSDL files and the web services they describe. UDDI itself uses SOAP to communicate and it is quite a universe in and of itself.

Classmaps

Now that we finally have WSDL in place, there is another interesting option available when instantiating the SOAP client and server objects: "classmap." This option can be used to explicitly map some WSDL types to PHP classes. It must be an array with WSDL types as keys and names of PHP classes as values.

An example should help to illustrate that. Suppose you have a web service that accepts orders. An individual order is represented by the class `Order`:

```
class Order
{
    public $productid;
    public $customerid;
    public $productcnt;

    public function __construct($productid, $customerid, $productcnt)
    {
        $this->productid  = $productid;
        $this->customerid = $customerid;
```

```
         $this->productcnt = $productcnt;
      }
   }

   class Orders
   {
      public $orders;
   }

   class Backend
   {
      public function placeOrders($orders)
      {
         return print_r($orders, 1); //just some debug info
      }
   }
```

Inside the WSDL there is an XSD entry defining an order:

```
<xsd:complexType name='Order'>
   <xsd:all>
      <xsd:element name='productid' type='xsd:string' />
      <xsd:element name='customerid' type='xsd:string' />
      <xsd:element name='productcnt' type='xsd:int' />
   </xsd:all>
</xsd:complexType>
```

There could also be another entry mentioning `Orders`. When launching the server, you can implement the "classmap" option like so:

```
$classmap = array('Order' => 'Order', 'Orders' => 'Orders');
$server = new SoapServer('soapserver3.wsdl', array('classmap' => $classmap));
$server->setClass("Backend");
$server->handle();
```

This will result in the SOAP client sending an array of `Order` objects and the SOAP server receiving that array of objects. Some code for the client side is displayed as follows, just suppose the classes `Order` and `Orders` are defined there too:

```
$classmap = array('Order' => 'Order','Orders' => 'Orders');
```

```
$client = new SoapClient('http://zfws/soapserver3.wsdl', array('classmap' =>
    $classmap));

$order1 = new Order(1,2,3);
$order2 = new Order(4,5,6);
$orders = new Orders();
$orders->orders = array($order1, $order2);

try {
   $classmap = array('Orders' => 'Orders','Order' => 'Order');
   $client = new SoapClient('http://zfws/soapserver3.wsdl', array('classmap' =>
       $classmap));
   echo $client->placeOrders($orders);
} catch (Exception $e) {
   echo $e->getMessage();
}
```

The last example will return the object as instantiated and interpreted by the `SoapServer`. This should give you a glimpse at what becomes possible in terms of the kinds of complex information that can be passed from the client to the server and back. Some highly advanced communication and web service solutions can be built using classmaps.

Error Handling

When a request results in an error, the `SoapServer` object can throw a `SoapFault` exception using it's `fault()` method. The most frequently used parameters for generating such a fault are a status code and a message string. This message string would contain some more explanation about the error encountered by the server code while handling the request. You can use this to create low-level error responses, for example when instantiating an object, which was supposed to be set as the SOAP server handler, fails:

```
<?php
$server = new SoapServer('somemath.wsdl');
try {
   $model = new WrongClassHere();
   $server->setObject($model);
   $server->handle();
```

```
   } catch (Exception $e) {
     $server->fault(001, "Error connecting to the web service backend");
   }
```

This will result in a `SoapFault` exception being thrown on the client side. A `SoapFault` can also be generated directly, bypassing `SoapServer::fault()`:

```
<?php
function createSomething($x)
{
   if ($error) {
      return new SoapFault("Sender", "Some error message");
   }
}

$server = new SoapServer(null, array('uri' => "http://example.com/"));
$server->addFunction("createSomething");
$server->handle();
```

In case the code inside the function detects an error or faulty response, it returns a SOAP fault instead of the expected response. `SoapFault` extends PHP's built-in `Exception` class, so it can be caught using a standard `try/catch` construct. Thus, a well-written SOAP client is able to understand and handle that fault response.

The code "Sender" used above is one of only a few legitimate "codes" that a SOAP fault can have. If another code is used, there is no guarantee the client will understand it. "Sender" and "Receiver" are legitimate and commonly used codes, as are "VersionMismatch", "MustUnderstand" and "DataEncodingUnknown". The W3 website[4] has more details. The two most commonly used codes for this purpose are "Sender" and "Receiver".

"Sender" is defined by the W3C as follows:

"The message was incorrectly formed or did not contain the appropriate information in order to succeed. For example, the message could lack the proper authentication or payment information. It is generally an indication that the message is not to be resent without change".

"Receiver" is defined as:

---
[4] http://www.w3.org/TR/soap12-part1/#faultcodes

"The message could not be processed for reasons attributable to the processing of the message rather than to the contents of the message itself. For example, processing could include communicating with an upstream SOAP node, which did not respond. The message could succeed if resent at a later point in time".

It is possible to prevent `SoapServer` using the default error handler by calling `use_soap_error_handler(true)`. The default value, "false", will prevent the `SoapServer` from propagating PHP errors to the client. Setting it to "true" will result in any errors in your code, which would not otherwise be shown, being sent as response to the client. In a development environment, setting this to "true" might save you some development and debugging time.

Error handling on the client side can be done by wrapping the `SoapClient` call in a `try/catch` block. Alternatively, setting the "exceptions" option to "false" prevents `SoapFault` exceptions being thrown by the client. Thus, if the server returned an error, the following code would handle the result and trigger a regular PHP error:

```php
<?php
$client = new SoapClient("http://example.com/some.wsdl", array('exceptions' =>
    false));
$result = $client->someFunction();
if (is_soap_fault($result)) {
   trigger_error("SOAP Fault: (faultcode: {$result->faultcode},
                 faultstring: {$result->faultstring})", E_USER_ERROR);
}
```

Wrapping the first two lines within a `try` block and catching the exception would have done the trick too, and should be the default way of handling this. Under certain circumstances however, you may prefer to skip exceptions being thrown in case of an error.

Debugging

During development and debugging, it can be very useful to be able to capture and inspect the raw SOAP messages being passed between client and server: in other words the contents of the SOAP envelopes, just like the examples we saw earlier in this chapter. Happily, there are some powerful tracing capabilities built into the `SoapClient` class:

- `__getLastRequest()`: returns the XML as sent
- `__getLastRequestHeaders()`: returns the SOAP headers as sent
- `__getLastResponse()`: returns the XML as received
- `__getLastResponseHeaders()`: returns the SOAP headers as received

All the return values are related to the last request sent and response received. For these methods to return data, it is necessary to add the "trace" option to the array passed to the `SoapClient`'s constructor. We can illustrate that by modifying some of our existing code:

```php
<?php

try {
   $client = new SoapClient(null, array('location' => "http://zfws/soapserver.
       php",
                                        'uri'      => "http://zfws/",
                                        'trace'    => true
   ));

   echo $client->someMathConstant('pi');
   echo '<pre>';
   var_dump($client->__getLastResponse());
   var_dump($client->__getLastResponseHeaders());
   var_dump($client->__getLastRequest());
   var_dump($client->__getLastRequestHeaders());
   echo '</pre>';
} catch (Exception $e) {
   echo $e->getMessage();
}
```

The output will show you the XML envelopes and headers involved in the SOAP calls, and the responses received by the SOAP client. For an even lower-level approach to this, see Appendix B on using the cURL extension for debugging.

If you want to debug incoming messages you can also use network package sniffing or grab and log the incoming request prior to handing it over to the SOAP server:

```php
<?php
```

```
$debug = true; // this will typically be dependent on the server environment

$input = file("php://input");
if ($debug) {
    error_log(PHP_EOL.date('Ymd H:i:s').' incoming: '.print_r($input,1),3,'/var/
        logs/some.log');
}

$input = implode(" ", $input);
$server = new SoapServer("somemath.wsdl");
$server->handle($input);
```

It is worth noting that it is typically recommended to keep the "trace" option turned off in production, as leaving it enabled can lead to large amounts of unnecessary data being held in memory, and this is especially true for busy SOAP services.

In WSDL mode, two further methods can be used to view information about the web service that was derived from parsing the WSDL file:

- __getTypes(): returns a list of the types defined in the WSDL

- __getFunctions(): returns a list of the operations defined in the WSDL, along with their method signatures

You can also use your browser's developer-friendly add-ons. Firefox has extensions which allow for inspecting request and response data, and of course there is the ultimate tool: Firebug. The latter allows you to inspect the request and response of every request made in Firefox, along with a plethora of other features. It is a valuable part of any developer's professional toolbox.

There are further developer-friendly tools, like SoapUI[5], a GUI tool for interfacing with SOAP services. SoapUI is an excellent piece of software that can speed up your development efforts considerably. There is a freely available version on the project's website; just download the install package for your platform and execute it. A wizard will guide you through the installation steps. Once installation is complete you can add a new project: just give it a name and point the project page to the WSDL file you created earlier. SoapUI creates test requests for you that you will be able to run instantly. Give it a try - it's invaluable for debugging and development purposes.

---

[5] http://www.soapui.org/

Finally, if you are working with remote .NET-based web services and you encounter issues like encoding, consider using a testing services[6].

SOAP and Zend Framework

The previous pages may perhaps have seemed dry and theoretical at points, but we are getting closer to our subject: using SOAP with Zend Framework, which has an excellent toolset for building SOAP servers and SOAP clients, and for WSDL generation. Even better, the Zend Framework reference manual has good explanations of the bits and pieces involved.

Zend_Soap_Client

Zend Framework not only provides a SOAP server library, it also offers you a client class that streamlines SOAP server access and wraps PHP's built-in SoapClient class. It can work in both WSDL and non-WSDL modes, and accepts an "options" array with key-value pairs that will be familiar to you from the various options we passed into SoapClient in previous examples.

Remember that you have to set a bunch of SOAP protocol options explicitly if working in non-WSDL mode. Whenever possible, stick to the WSDL approach.

Zend_Soap_Server

The SOAP server component of Zend Framework wraps PHP's SoapServer and builds on top of Zend_Server, as do Zend_Rest_Server, Zend_XmlRpc_Server and some other server components. This results in a SOAP server component that behaves consistently with the rest of the server components in Zend Framework, while allowing use of all the existing features of SoapServer. It is a mature component, and can be very powerful when combined with WSDL auto-discovery.

Of course, you can do a lot of what Zend_Soap_Server does all by yourself, if you're one who likes to reinvent the wheel. You could begin with the following simple example:

---

[6] http://www.mssoapinterop.org

```php
<?php

class Customsoap extends SoapServer
{
    public function __construct($wsdl = NULL, $options = array())
    {
        parent::__construct($wsdl, $options);
    }
}

require_once('./Mta_Service.php');

$soapserver = new Customsoap('./service.wsdl');
$soapserver->setClass('Mta_Service');
$soapserver->handle();

?>
```

This is indeed all it takes to extend PHP's `SoapServer`. You could take this as a starting point and try to implement all the features of `Zend_Soap_Server` or other web service libraries. On the other hand, `Zend_Soap_Server` is ready for use, tested and mature, and it provides you with:

- built-in error and exception handling
- input checks for incoming requests, for example a check for valid XML as input
- a powerful combination when used with `Zend_Soap_AutoDiscover`

To provide an example: `Zend_Soap_Server` reads its input from `php://stdin` and checks whether the incoming request is a well-formed XML structure by attempting to parse it using `DOMDocument::loadXML()` before handing it over to a `SoapServer` instance. This simple-but-neat trick allows for nice exception handling in case of a failing request.

`Zend_Soap_Server` can work in WSDL and non-WSDL mode and accepts about every option available in PHP's `SoapServer`. Simply pass an "options" array as second argument when constructing your SOAP server, just like we did before when exploring the `SoapServer` class.

Zend_Soap_Wsdl

Zend_Soap_Wsdl is used internally by Zend_Soap_Server, and can be used to decode WSDL files. You can also use it to *create* a fully featured WSDL file, complete with methods for adding bindings, portTypes, operations and services.

Zend_Soap_Wsdl handles native PHP primitive types like string, integer, float and boolean, and maps them to their XML Schema counterparts: xsd:string, xsd:int, xsd:float, xsd:boolean. PHP's "void" is mapped to an empty type. More complex, non-scalar, structures such as PHP arrays and objects are mapped to soap-enc:Array and xsd:struct respectively.

How PHP classes are mapped to types depends on what is known as a "complexType strategy," which is used for interpreting the given code. Each PHP class to be passed in the SOAP message will result in a xsd:complexType, and sometimes an xsd:sequence, being defined and added to the WSDL file. By default, the Zend_Soap_Wsdl_Strategy_DefaultComplexType strategy is used for detection and for the building of WSDL files. However, alternative strategies are available. These are the available strategies and how they handle the mapping:

- **Zend_Soap_Wsdl_Strategy_DefaultComplexType**: uses reflection to iterate over the public attributes of the PHP class, and uses these attributes as subtypes of the complex object type

- **Zend_Soap_Wsdl_Strategy_AnyType**: interprets every complex type as xsd:anyType. This is quick and easy, and tends to work well with PHP-based SOAP clients. Clients developed in other languages may require a more detailed description of the complexType however, and may fail on this

- **Zend_Soap_Wsdl_Strategy_ArrayOfTypeSequence**: this strategy detects return values of the type int[], string[] and other sequence types (booleans, floats, objects and even nested arrays of objects)

- **Zend_Soap_Wsdl_Strategy_ArrayOfTypeComplex**: detects arrays of objects. Object types are detected using Zend_Soap_Wsdl_Strategy_DefaultComplexType and wrapped in an array

- **Zend_Soap_Wsdl_Strategy_Composite**: This strategy can combine all strategies by using a typemap passed to it in the form of an array with `$type => $strategy` mapping

If a type cannot be mapped, then `xsd:anyType` is used. Don't worry if the above seems overly complex: we will shortly see an example which will clear things up.

`Zend_Soap_Wsdl` parses and maps types using PHP's reflection features and, perhaps more importantly, information found in docblocks. It is extremely important for correct type detection that you take great care to correctly specify `@param` and `@return` values in the docblocks for your class methods.

Zend_Soap_AutoDiscover

This class will probably make you fall in love with Zend Framework's SOAP components, after seeing how simple it makes it to create a decent WSDL file. `Zend_Soap_AutoDiscover` allows for complete and robust auto-generation of a WSDL file. Ideally, it takes the same class or object that has been used for creating the SOAP server as input and parses it, using `Zend_Soap_Wsdl` and thus PHP's reflection features. The docblock comments and, more specifically, the tags defining the method parameters and return values are used for determining the input and output for each exposed method. It is a convenient and powerful tool for constructing WSDL files.

Let's have another look at a previous example where we defined the `Order` class, and where we passed a classmap to the client and server to define more complex parameters. How did we create that WSDL file for that example? In fact we did it using `Zend_Soap_AutoDiscover`. All it takes for the classes to be picked up as required by the discovery magic is adding the correct information in docblocks:

```php
<?php

class Order
{
    /** @var string */
    public $productid;
    /** @var string */
    public $customerid;
    /** @var int */
    public $productcnt;
```

```
    public function __construct($productid, $customerid, $productcnt)
    {
        $this->productid  = $productid;
        $this->customerid = $customerid;
        $this->productcnt = $productcnt;
    }
}


class Orders
{
    /** @var Order[] */
    public $orders;
}


class Backend
{
    /**
     * @param Orders $orders
     * @return string
     */
    public function placeOrders($orders)
    {
        return print_r($orders, true);
    }
}

//some Zend Application and include path stuff omitted
//...

$autodiscover = new Zend_Soap_AutoDiscover('
    Zend_Soap_Wsdl_Strategy_ArrayOfTypeComplex');

$autodiscover->setClass('Backend');
$autodiscover->setUri('http://zfws/soapserver3.php');
$autodiscover->handle();
```

In this way, we can generate WSDL out-of-the-box, with no hand coding and no cursing. We specified `Zend_Soap_Wsdl_Strategy_ArrayOfTypeComplex` as the strategy needed for parsing our `Order[]` docblock entry in class `Orders`. The default strategy `Zend_Soap_Wsdl_Strategy_DefaultComplexType` would have thrown us an error, but still could have been used were it not for those specific docblock entries.

So, docblocks aren't just good practice, they become vital if more complex WSDL files need to be created. In case you are wondering, the phpDocumentor[7] site provides detailed and comprehensive documentation on docblocks and their usage. And remember, there is a "gotcha" you might miss when looking at why your autodiscovery may not work: the docblocks must begin with /** and not /*. PHP's reflection, used internally by the autodiscovery mechanism, will miss on the /* and it might cost you significant time tracking that down if you aren't aware of it.

Note that the PHPUnit testing framework can take advantage of docblock information too, as it can semi-automatically create tests using information found in docblocks.

Removing the docblocks and using Zend_Soap_Wsdl_Strategy_DefaultComplexType works too, but the WSDL generated as a result is far less informative than the one we created in our example. In case you need more complex combinations, use Zend_Soap_Wsdl_Strategy_Composite, which allows for a strategy definition per type found.

One last point about WSDL and Zend_Soap_AutoDiscover that we didn't yet mention is that Zend_Soap_AutoDiscover offers support for different transport mechanisms and encoding styles for the resulting WSDL. The default style is "rpc" and default encoding is "encoded." We will not go into too much detail on this, but it is another aspect of the versatility of the Zend Framework SOAP component.

Example Code

Let's get some work done using Zend Framework. We're going to revisit some of our previous examples, using the class we prepared for MTA. Remember, we're still doing all this for a purpose. Let's launch the SOAP server:

```
// ... some include path stuff omitted ...

ini_set("soap.wsdl_cache_enabled", 0); //for development

if (isset($_GET['WSDL'])) {
    $autodiscover = new Zend_Soap_AutoDiscover();
    Zend_Loader::loadClass('Mta_Service');
    $autodiscover->setClass('Mta_Service');
```

---
[7] http://www.phpdoc.org/

```
    $autodiscover->setUri('http://zfws/SOAP.php');
    $autodiscover->handle();
} else {
    $options = array('soap_version' => SOAP_1_2);
    Zend_Loader::loadClass('Mta_Service');
    $server = new Zend_Soap_Server('http://zfws/SOAP.php?WSDL=1', $options);
    $server->setObject(new Mta_Service());
    $server->handle();
}
```

The WSDL info is created on the fly if the "WSDL" GET parameter is defined.

Where do you place all this code typically? One option is to copy the `public/index.php` file (containing the `Zend_Application` bootstrap code from Chapter 1 to `SOAP.php` for the server and leave out the lines that launch the MVC components. Just add the code to launch the SOAP server instead, and off you go. As an alternative you could create a separate controller, or even a separate module for web services in a broader application, and put the SOAP server and magic WSDL generation code in there, in separate action methods.

Option 1: Separate Bootstrap Code in a Separate PHP File

Suppose you place the soap server code and WSDL generation part in `/zfws/SOAP.php`. If you're running Apache with `mod_rewrite` (or indeed nginx or lighttpd with some rewrite rules), then you could rewrite `/zfws/WSDL` to `/zfws/SOAP.php?WSDL`. Both URLs would launch only the necessary code for their respective purposes and thus would be nice and simple.

This is a simple solution with practically no overhead, which is desirable when creating an API that will be consumed by many clients. If you're a speed freak and dislike unnecessary overhead, then you'll stick to this option.

A further advantage when using a separate file is that you can easily map version numbers of your API to different files, or to the same file but using additional parameters. If, for example, you have two versions of the API, 1.0 and 1.2, then you could URL rewrite the URLs `/SOAP/v1.0` or `/v1.0/SOAP` to `SOAP.php?v=1.0`.

Option 2: Wrap it Inside a Controller

You could alternatively place the SOAP server and WSDL code in a separate Zend Framework controller as follows:

```php
<?php

class SoapController extends Zend_Controller_Action
{
   public function init()
   {
      //... some init stuff for your controller ...
   }

   public function indexAction()
   {
      //... here you could output some information about your service ...
   }

   public function soapAction()
   {
      if (APPLICATION_ENV == 'development') {
         ini_set("soap.wsdl_cache_enabled", 0); //for development
      }
      $options = array('soap_version' => SOAP_1_2);
      Zend_Loader::loadClass('Mta_Service');
      $server = new Zend_Soap_Server('http://zfws/soap/soap', $options);
      $server->setObject(new Mta_Service());
      $server->handle();
   }

   public function wsdlAction()
   {
      if (APPLICATION_ENV == 'development') {
         ini_set("soap.wsdl_cache_enabled", 0);//for development
      }
      $autodiscover = new Zend_Soap_AutoDiscover();
      $autodiscover->setClass('Mta_Service');
      $autodiscover->setUri('http://zfws/soap/wsdl');
      $autodiscover->handle();
   }
}
```

If you think this fits better with the rest of your application, for example if there is more to your application than just the web service, you might find it more appropriate to organize the code in this way. Some of the objects and tools that you might have made available through regular MVC creation, such as plugins, helpers, registry objects, models and your DB layer, would be available instantly, and so this could be a very appealing solution at first glance. Zend_Application can be bootstrapped in a separate file too, however, as we saw in option 1, and in the end there aren't many reasons to choose a separate controller with SOAP code.

Placing your code in a separate bootstrap file is probably the best option anyway. You can even combine multiple web service endpoints into one boostrap file. For example:

```
// ... some Zend_Application stuff...

switch ($_GET['service']) {
   case 'xmlrpc':
       $bsinfo = array('class' => 'XmlRpc_Bootstrap',
                       'path'  => APPLICATION_PATH . '/ServiceBootstrap.php');
       break;
   case 'soap':
  $bsinfo = array('class' => 'Soap_Bootstrap',
                       'path'  => APPLICATION_PATH . '/ServiceBootstrap.php');
       break;
}

/** Zend_Application */
require_once 'Zend/Application.php';

$app = new Zend_Application(
           APPLICATION_ENV,
           array(
               'bootstrap' => $bsinfo,
               'config' => APPLICATION_PATH . '/configs/application.ini',
           )
       );
$app->bootstrap()
    ->run();
```

The contents of the ServiceBootstrap.php class file:

```
class Soap_Bootstrap extends Bootstrap
```

```
{
    public function run()
    {
        if (isset($_GET['WSDL'])) {
            $autodiscover = new Zend_Soap_AutoDiscover();
            Zend_Loader::loadClass('Mta_Service');
            $autodiscover->setClass('Mta_Service');
            $autodiscover->setUri('http://zfws/API.php?service=soap');
            $autodiscover->handle();
        } else {
            $options = array('soap_version' => SOAP_1_2);
            Zend_Loader::loadClass('Mta_Service');
            $server = new Zend_Soap_Server('http://zfws/API.php?service=soap&WSDL
                =1', $options);
            $server->setObject(new Mta_Service());
            $server->handle();
        }
    }
}
```

Finally, you can test the newly created SOAP server and WSDL file using `Zend_Soap_Client`, by pointing a `Zend_Soap_Client` instance at the URL of the WSDL file, and starting to talk to the available operations:

```
$client = new Zend_Soap_Client("http://zfws/soap/wsdl",
                              array('soap_version' => SOAP_1_2));
```

A call to `http://zfws/soap/wsdl` will test the SOAP service and WSDL file as launched from a controller. A call to `http://zfws/SOAP.php?wsdl=1` will talk to our SOAP service in a separate bootstrap file.

`http://zfws/API.php?service=soap&WSDL=1` will talk to a SOAP class being launched through another bootstrap file, `API.php`, where we will add other web service options later on.

Extending Zend_Soap

Apart from the WSDL generation and its tremendous power, there are further advantages to using `Zend_Soap_Server` instead of the native `SoapServer` class. For example, you can extend the class and implement some pre- or post-request operations.

In addition `Zend_Soap_Server` allows for plain XML as the request format, but also supports objects being passed as a request. Objects of the following types are converted to XML by `Zend_Soap_Server` if passed as the request:

- `DOMDocument`

- `DOMNode` - here, the parent `DOMDocument` will be located and converted to XML

- `SimpleXMLElement`

A generic `stdClass` instance can also be passed as the request object and its `__toString()` method will be called. Again, the output will be verified to be valid XML prior to processing.

Parsing the `Zend_Soap_Server` output before handing it back to the SOAP client is also possible. Just set the return response property using `$server->setReturnResponse(true);` and `Zend_Soap_Server::handle()` will return output that you can manipulate some more instead of just sending the response directly to the output stream.

By way of an example, you could use request and response processing to log all incoming and outgoing XML while you are developing. The log file would become cluttered, but it might help you during debugging.

Another example might be the creation of a low-level blacklist to restrict the calling of certain methods to clients from specific IP addresses. This is a low-level approach and something that might be better solved using `Zend_Acl` and API keys, as we will see in the next chapters.

A more realistic scenario for pre-parsing the incoming request might be to impose rate limits to prevent excessive calls coming from the same IP. This might be something that you want to check with some basic code first, eventually even avoiding setting up the SOAP server and thus lowering memory usage on the server.

Now let's actually extend `Zend_Soap_Server` by creating `MTA_Soap_Server`, and place some of the examples for pre- and post-request handling in our newly created class:

```php
<?php

require_once 'Zend/Server/Interface.php';
require_once 'Zend/Soap/Server.php';
```

```php
class Mta_Soap_Server extends Zend_Soap_Server
{
    public function __construct($wsdl = null, array $options = null)
    {
        parent::__construct($wsdl, $options);
    }

    /**
     * Handle a request by overriding the default ZF handle() method
     *
     * @param string $request Optional request
     * @return void|string
     */
    public function handle($request = null)
    {
        if (null === $request) {
            $request = file_get_contents('php://input');
        }

        if ($this->checkAllow($_SERVER['REMOTE_ADDR'])) {
            error_log(PHP_EOL.date('Ymd h:i:s')
                . " REQUEST: "
                . print_r($request, 1), 3, '/tmp/webservice.log');
            parent::handle($request);
            $response = parent::getLastResponse();
            error_log(PHP_EOL.date('Ymd h:i:s')
                . " RESPONSE: "
                . print_r($response, 1), 3, '/tmp/webservice.log');
            return $response;
        } else {
            //log limit exceeded for given IP

            //return SOAP fault
            $soap = $this->_getSoap();
            $soap->fault(509 , 'Limit Exceeded');
        }
    }

    /**
     * Check if this IP isn't firing too many requests
     *
     * @param string $ip
     * @return bool
     */
```

```
    protected function checkAllow($ip)
    {
       //do check, in db for example
       //and if limit exceeded return false

       //else
       return true;
    }
}
```

We accept the incoming request, perform a check on whether the caller has exceeded his limit, log the request and response SOAP envelopes, and finally return the result. If you change `checkAllow()` to return `false`, you'll end up with a `SoapFault` response being received by the SOAP client.

In the next chapters, we will also show you when extending `Zend_Soap_AutoDiscover` might become an interesting option.

Public and Private Web Services

Before moving on to discuss API keys and the use of `Zend_Acl` for more refined access control, there is also another, simpler approach for distinguishing between private and public parts of the web service. You could create a separate `SOAP.php` bootstrap file or separate controller, depending on how you set up your SOAP server for public access.

In case of a separate bootstrap file, the directory layout may look like this:

```
/path/to/web/html
    |-- public
    |    |-- SOAP.php
    |    '-- WSDL.php
    |-- private
         |-- SOAP.php
         '-- WSDL.php
```

Instead of the proposed directory layout, you could also place all code in a single file and add some URL rewrite magic to map, for example, /SOAP/private to SOAP.php?mode=private and /SOAP/private/wsdl SOAP.php?mode=private&wsdl=1. You get the picture.

All in all, this may not be the most robust solution, but if you're not looking any further than that and this serves your needs, why not? Remember, KISS[8]. Access to the private SOAP server may then be restricted to certain IP addresses, or you could enforce the use of authentication headers for the incoming requests and check for a valid username and password combination. The client could insert a SOAP header with user credentials. On the server side, these credentials could be checked before handing the XML over to the `Zend_Soap_Server` instance.

An alternative approach is to define a public authentication method which accepts a username and password. If authorized, return a generated token with limited lifetime. On each request made to the private web service, this token will have to be sent along. Our custom `Mta_Soap_Server` can strip the token out, check it and hand the request over to `Zend_Soap_Server`.

Logging, Versioning, Response and Error Codes

Optional logging, the use of a version number for your web service and clear error codes and response codes are things you may not consider crucial whenever you start building your web service. But if done right they can save you and anyone working with your web service a lot of time.

Logging

Logging requests and responses, or at the least the incoming request parameters for the methods, may help you when troubleshooting problems on a production machine. You might even consider an optional parameter in every request that allows for more verbose logging. When debugging for example, you could use this to tell the server to log the entire request and response envelopes, or even entire database queries or other backend calls. Handling and stripping out that logging parameter could be done during the pre-processing of the request.

Versioning

Suppose you have a fully working SOAP service running at a URI such as `http://webservice.marble-toys.com/SOAP`. It is running fine and handles thousands

---

[8]http://en.wikipedia.org/wiki/KISS_principle

of requests without a problem. At a certain point in time MTA decides to improve the web service and allow for a number of additional methods to be exposed. Some existing ones will change slightly and these changes will not be backwards compatible. The existing URI should remain the same however. How can you manage this without breaking too much and without having to contact everyone using your service to change the URI they use?

You could have thought of this when you started of course, using a URL scheme along the lines of `http://webservice.marble-toys.com/v1/SOAP` instead. As an alternative, we could use and pre-process a version parameter in every request, as we did with the logging flag before. Then we would load the correct class for that version: easy and simple.

Requests without a version specified could be handled as requests to the first version using URL rewrites and defaulting to version 1 in your code. An example that tries to handle this might look like so:

```
// ...

$version = parseVersionFromUri();
$serverversions = array('1', '1.2', '1.2');
if (in_array($version,$serversions)) {
   include('/some/path/' . $version . '/Mta_Service.php');
} else {
   //return a SOAP fault stating that there is no such version
}
```

Error Codes

Returning useful and meaningful error codes will be something other developers will thank you for. It makes it easier for them to work with your web service and to debug their code. It will also decrease the number of calls to your support desk.

For example:

- 403: Access forbidden
- 509: Limit exceeded

And so on. You can try to reuse well known error codes such as the ones returned in HTTP responses, or mimic well known web services like those at Amazon and

Google. Whatever you choose, provide a list of possible error codes and what they mean somewhere on your API documentation site.

You can even extend it and return not only error codes, but response codes as well. For example:

- 200: Ok - when just returning requested info

- 201: Created - when an insert in the database has finished successfully

These can be added in the SOAP headers or the body of the response.

While you are at it, you might add an `echo()` method to each web service you create. The only thing such a method should do is reply with the exact request as received by the server. This allows a remote developer, or even your own monitoring system, to check that what the client sends to you is received and seen by the SOAP server as expected.

Summary

We managed to cover a wide range of SOAP-related theory and examples in this chapter. The material covered included:

- an overview of most of the SOAP-related concepts necessary for your daily SOAP needs

- plain PHP SOAP calls and server side code

- WSDL for describing our SOAP service and why it is helpful

- most of the SOAP-related Zend Framework components including the powerful `Zend_Soap_Wsdl` and `Zend_Soap_AutoDiscover` components

Finally, our code is approaching an actual solution to support MTA's needs.

Chapter 4

Customizing Our SOAP Service

Introduction

We found that MTA wanted its web service to be a closed service for the most part. How can we achieve that? We saw an example using authentication headers in the SOAP request, but what if we want something dead simple, with less coding required on the client side? We could use a secret token known only to the client and the server. This token or key is often called an API key, so let's stick to that name. Requiring an API key can be done in several different ways.

Solution 1: Add an API Key Parameter to Each Method

We could solve this in a quick and dirty fashion by rewriting the class, to require an additional parameter to be passed to every method, as in the following example:

```
class Mta_Service
{
   /**
    * @param int $customer_id Customer identifier
    * @return array|object
    */
   public function getCatalogue($apikey, $customer_id, $category = '*')
   {
      if ($this->hasAccess($apikey, __FUNCTION__) {
```

```
        Zend_Loader::loadFile(APPLICATION_PATH . '/models/Product.php');
        $catalogue = new Mta_Model_Product();
        return $catalogue->getItems($customer_id, $category);
    } else {
        return false;
    }
}

// other methods omitted for brevity
}
```

Pro and Cons

The above is not ideal, as it would cause considerable maintenance issues. Adding the API key as the first parameter for each method renders the class and its methods significantly harder to use if used outside of a web service context. You don't want to be required to pass API keys when talking to this class directly from application code, for example, and future code reuse should always be on your checklist. Plus, there is no real clean solution for returning a SOAP error if access is denied, unless you return a `SoapFault`, which means even more SOAP specific code in a class that you might want to use for other purposes.

In addition, the code actually checking the access on the method using the supplied API key is duplicated inside each and every method involved. As soon as you change something at this level, you will need to check and change code everywhere in the web service classes. Unnecessary duplication of code is considered bad practice and should be avoided if possible.

Suppose you want to restrict access for a certain API key to a certain source IP address; that would mean scanning through several files and fixing things at several locations, all with an increased risk of introducing new bugs at the same time.

This solution doesn't stand up in the long run, that much is clear. Checking access to methods should be concentrated in a single place in the code flow, where it will be easy to change the logic involved if required. Checking access *before* the method is actually called would be even better in terms of performance, since it would avoid unnecessary calls to parts of the code.

Solution 2: Pre-parse the SOAP Message

We could decide to tackle the problem during an earlier stage of the request-response chain. Why not check the incoming XML to see if it contains an API key? We could then validate that key and strip it out of the envelope. The resulting XML string could then be passed to the web service, which does not then have to be changed.

Let's take another look at our custom `Mta_Soap_Server` and adapt the `handle()` method to perform the API key check. For readability, the code handling the request/response logging has been omitted here:

```
public function handle($request = null)
{
   if (null === $request) {
      $request = file_get_contents('php://input');
   }

   if ($this->_checkAllow($_SERVER['REMOTE_ADDR'])) {
      $dom = new DOMDocument();
      if (!$dom->loadXML($request)) {
         throw new Zend_Soap_Server_Exception('Invalid XML');
      } else {
         //strip out api_key stuff
         $xml = simplexml_load_string($request);

         $url = 'http://' . $_SERVER['HTTP_HOST'] . $_SERVER['REQUEST_URI'];

         $children = (array) $xml->children('http://schemas.xmlsoap.org/soap/
             envelope/')
                              ->Body
                              ->children($url);
         $methods = array_keys($children);
         $method  = $methods[0];

         $soap = $this->_getSoap();

         $apikey = (string) $xml->children('http://schemas.xmlsoap.org/soap/
             envelope/')
                              ->Body
                              ->children($url)
                              ->{$method}
                              ->children()
                              ->apikey;
```

66 ■ Customizing Our SOAP Service

```
            if ($this->_hasAccess($apikey,$method)) {
                //strip api info
                unset($xml->children('http://schemas.xmlsoap.org/soap/envelope/')
                        ->Body
                        ->children($url)
                        ->{$method}
                        ->children()
                        ->apikey);

                $request = $xml->asXml();

                //remove whitespace & empty lines
                $request = trim($request);
                $request = preg_replace("/(^[\r\n]*|[\r\n]+)[\s\t]*[\r\n]+/", "\n",
                    $request);
                parent::handle($request);
                $response = parent::getLastResponse();
            } else {
                $soap = $this->_getSoap();
                $soap->fault(403 , 'Access forbidden');
            }
        }

        return $response;
    } else {
        //log limit exceeded for given IP

        //return SOAP fault
        $soap = $this->_getSoap();
        $soap->fault(509 , 'Limit Exceeded');
    }
}
```

Here we check the XML using `DomDocument`, just as `Zend_Soap_Server` does, and then we load the message using `simplexml_load_string()`. We navigate through the `SimpleXMLElement` object to determine the method called, and to retrieve the API key used. A protected method named `_hasAccess()` can perform a check, such as a database lookup, to find out if the API key actually has access.

If access is granted, we remove the key from the XML object, cast it to a string and strip out resulting whitespace prior to handing the request object over to `Zend_Soap_Server`.

Customizing Our SOAP Service ■ 67

This strategy does have some impact on WSDL generation, since we're expecting the clients of our web service to know that they have to send an API key with each request. This means that we will have to adapt the WSDL file accordingly. We can do so by extending the Zend_Soap_Autodiscover class and overriding _addFunctionToWsdl(). The entire code held within _addFunctionToWsdl() is quite large, so this example shows a trimmed version with our changes only:

```php
class Mta_Soap_AutoDiscover extends Zend_Soap_AutoDiscover
{
    // this is the parameter to be added, more additional
    // parameters can be defined here
    private $_extra_params = array('apikey' => 'string');

    public function __construct($strategy = true, $uri=null)
    {
        parent::__construct($strategy, $uri);
    }

    /**
     * overload the ZF method
     * ...
     */
    protected function _addFunctionToWsdl($function, $wsdl, $port, $binding)
    {
        $uri = $this->getUri();

        // ...

        // Add the input message (parameters)
        $args = array();
        if ($this->_bindingStyle['style'] == 'document') {
            // Document style: wrap all parameters in a sequence element
            $sequence = array();
            // here we insert the extra params like API key
            foreach ($this->_extra_params as $param_name => $param_type) {
                $sequenceElement = array(
                    'name' => $param_name,
                    'type' => $wsdl->getType($param_type)
                );
                if (in_array($param_name, $this->_extra_optional)) {
                    $sequenceElement['nillable'] = 'true';
                }
                $sequence[] = $sequenceElement;
            }
```

```
            // ...here the actual parameters are added to $sequence...

            $element = array(
                'name' => $function->getName(),
                'sequence' => $sequence
            );
            // Add the wrapper element part, which must be named 'parameters'
            $args['parameters'] = array('element' => $wsdl->addElement($element));
        } else {
            // RPC style: add each parameter as a typed part
            // here we insert the extra params like API key
            foreach ($this->_extra_params as $param_name => $param_type) {
                $args[$param_name] = array('type' => $wsdl->getType($param_type));
            }
            // ...here the actual parameters are added...
        }
        // ...and the rest of the WSDL is built...
    }
}
```

The extended class looks daunting, but the only thing we did was add an additional parameter, which is going to be added to the WSDL file, alongside the others which were found using reflection by Zend_Soap autodiscovery. We defined the type "string" for the extra parameter "apikey", something you may have overlooked. You can add additional parameters like "apikey", just take care to pick the correct PHP type.

Pros and Cons

This is a clean solution. It separates different duties and handles the API check early in the request flow. It took some customizing however. On the other hand, you would need to do this only once, even if you grow from one to many web services. No changes were necessary to our actual class Mta_Service, and the resulting WSDL file defines the additional API key for each method.

An example call might look as follows:

```
<soapenv:Envelope xmlns:xsi="http://www.w3.org/2001/XMLSchema-instance" xmlns:
    xsd="http://www.w3.org/2001/XMLSchema" xmlns:soapenv="http://schemas.xmlsoap
    .org/soap/envelope/" xmlns:soap="http://zfws/SOAP.php">
    <soapenv:Header/>
    <soapenv:Body>
```

```
        <soap:createOrder soapenv:encodingStyle="http://schemas.xmlsoap.org/soap/
            encoding/">
          <apikey xsi:type="xsd:string">wrongkey</apikey>
          <product_id xsi:type="xsd:int">1</product_id>
          <customer_id xsi:type="xsd:int">1</customer_id>
          <productcnt xsi:type="xsd:int">1</productcnt>
        </soap:createOrder>
    </soapenv:Body>
</soapenv:Envelope>
```

This call will result in this response:

```
<SOAP-ENV:Envelope xmlns:SOAP-ENV="http://schemas.xmlsoap.org/soap/envelope/">
    <SOAP-ENV:Body>
        <SOAP-ENV:Fault>
            <faultcode>403</faultcode>
            <faultstring>Access forbidden</faultstring>
        </SOAP-ENV:Fault>
    </SOAP-ENV:Body>
</SOAP-ENV:Envelope>
```

You just have to make sure that the server itself uses the WSDL that reflects the actual `Mta_Service` class, not the manipulated output created by `Mta_Soap_AutoDiscover`. `SOAP.php` has to be adapted to look like so:

```
if (isset($_GET['WSDL'])) {
    $autodiscover = new Mta_Soap_AutoDiscover();
    $autodiscover->setClass('Mta_Service');
    $autodiscover->setUri('http://zfws/SOAP.php');
    $autodiscover->handle();
} elseif (isset($_GET['INTERNALWSDL'])) {
    $autodiscover = new Zend_Soap_AutoDiscover();
    $autodiscover->setClass('Mta_Service');
    $autodiscover->setUri('http://zfws/SOAP.php');
    $autodiscover->handle();
} else {
    $options = array('soap_version' => SOAP_1_2);
    $server = new Mta_Soap_Server('http://zfws/SOAP.php?INTERNALWSDL=1', $options
        );
    $server->setObject(new Mta_Service());
    $server->handle();
}
```

Solution 3: Use Magic Methods

Another solution we could try out is to implement the API key authentication using calls to the "magic" methods introduced in PHP5. Suppose you have a class that looks like this:

```
class ExampleClass
{
   public function __call($name, $arguments)
   {
      echo "We do not support {$name} in " . __CLASS__;
   }
}
</code>

If you were not familiar with the "magic" behavior of ''__call()'', you might
    expect a method invocation like this to fail with a fatal error:

<code>
$object = new ExampleClass();
$object->nonExistingMethod();
```

However, this instead outputs "We do not support nonExistingMethod in ExampleClass". So __call() is used as a special kind of fallback method, and is triggered if a non-existing method is called. Inside __call() you could throw an Exception, or try to forward the call, including the arguments, to another method, or even to another object. A sister method, __callStatic(), is triggered when inaccessible methods are called in a static context.

While __call() and __callStatic() are used for overloading inaccessible methods, __set() and __unset() are used for overloading inaccessible properties. They are used for getting and setting otherwise inaccessible data, such as class properties that were declared private. By doing so, you could add some checks on which properties you would allow to be added or retrieved from your objects. Two more overloading methods are left here: __isset() and __unset(). The first is used when isset() or empty() is issued against an inaccessible property, the latter for unsetting an inaccessible property.

Another interesting magic method is __toString(). This method will determine how a class will react if it is treated as a string, for example as an argument to echo().

Inside __toString(), an object could generate and return an XML representation of itself, for example, and thus echoing or printing the object would result in an XML string being displayed.

With that behind us, let's now break down the solution we are considering here into smaller pieces. For an example using magic methods:

```php
class Mta_Servicewrapper
{
   /**
    * @param string $method_name The name of the inaccessible method called
    * @param array $arguments The arguments that were passed to that method
    */
   public function __call($method_name, $arguments)
   {
      $service = new Mta_Service();
      if (method_exists($service, $method_name)) {
         if ($this->_hasAccess($arguments[0], $method_name)) {
            unset($arguments[0]);
            return call_user_func_array(array($service, $method_name),
               $arguments);
         } else {
            return new SoapFault('Sender', '403 : Access forbidden');
         }
      } else {
         return new SoapFault('Sender', '404 : Service not found');
      }
   }

   /**
    * Check if API key has access to method
    *
    * @param string $apikey
    * @param string $method
    * @return boolean
    */
   protected function _hasAccess($apikey, $method)
   {
      // if API key has no access, return false
      if ((string) $apikey != 'correctkey') {
         return false;
      }
      // else
      return true;
   }
```

}

Then, in our bootstrap file (SOAPbis.php, we use the newly created wrapper class instead of Mta_Service:

```php
<?php

//... some Zend_Application and include stuff ...

ini_set("soap.wsdl_cache_enabled", 0); // for development

if (isset($_GET['WSDL'])) {
   $autodiscover = new Mta_Soap_AutoDiscover();
   $autodiscover->setClass('Mta_Service');
   $autodiscover->setUri('http://zfws/SOAPbis.php');
   $autodiscover->handle();
} else {
   $options = array('soap_version' => SOAP_1_2);
   $server = new Zend_Soap_Server('http://zfws/SOAPbis.php?WSDL=1', $options);
   $server->setClass('Mta_Servicewrapper');
   $server->handle();
}
```

The Mta_Servicewrapper class will forward calls to Mta_Service if access is granted, given the received API key and method accessed.

Just as in our previous solution, we need the clients to be aware that there is an API key required for each method, so we must remember to use our previously created Mta_Soap_Autodiscover class for WSDL generation.

Pros and Cons

This seems to be a clean solution which allows for heavy modification of the incoming request, without extending Zend_Soap_Server. One argument against it is that the API key is now expected to be the first argument, while in the second solution, that was not an issue. Another disadvantage is that this solution does not allow response logging to happen *inside* Mta_Servicewrapper. On the other hand, response logging could be done in the bootstrap file, SOAPbis.php, instead.

Making your choice between this and the previous solution largely depends on your project, the requirements and your personal taste.

Summary

- We know how to extend Zend_Soap

- We added some debug logging and rate limiting checks

- We extended Zend_Soap_Server and Zend_Soap_Autodiscover to allow for additional parameter beyond the ones derived from the API class

Deliverables:

- We now have an API key that can be used to check and restrict access per method

Chapter 5

REST

Introduction

Our customer wanted support for more than one web service methodology, remember? We already talked a lot about SOAP, but there are more techniques available when exposing an API. REST is very popular and very useful, so let's have a closer look.

Some Background on REST

Representational State Transfer (REST) is often described as an architectural style or pattern. REST communication is established between client and server, just like SOAP. REST however, does not describe a complete protocol, nor does it require an endless list of specifications. It is not a standard governed by some official body, but rather consists of a collection of principles.

The central concept of REST is that of the "resource" - some coherent item or collection of information that is of value and interest to someone. This is roughly analogous to an object in object-oriented systems. URIs are mapped to resources, so that each resource is uniquely identified by a URI. Clients perform HTTP requests against those URIs, with the intended behavior being defined by the HTTP request method.

Thus, HTTP methods such as PUT, POST, GET and DELETE are the verbs that define what should happen to the resources being queried, and a URI referring to a single resource, such as `http://zfws/rest/orders/12`, should respond to HTTP verbs as follows:

- GET: retrieves the detailed data - a "representation" - of the member of the collection of orders referred to by its ID, in this case "12"
- POST: saves the data being submitted with the request as a child of the resource referred to in the URI. This effectively turns the resource referred to into a collection of resources. The order could turn into an order encompassing other orders
- PUT: updates or replaces the resource in the collection
- DELETE: deletes the member from the collection, thus removes the order from the list of orders

A URI pointing to a list of elements, dubbed a collection, such as `http://zfws/rest/orders` should respond as follows:

- GET: retrieves the data for the entire collection or set of orders
- POST: adds a member to the collection, in this case creating an order. Usually the new ID assigned by the system is returned as part of the data sent in response
- PUT: replaces the entire collection with the data being sent
- DELETE: deletes the entire collection

A REST service need not implement all possible combinations. You may for example not like the idea of someone overwriting your entire list of orders, nor does it necessarily make sense for orders to have a notion of child orders. In a situation where resources can have child nodes however, you may wish to support POST for a resource URI. It is up to you to select the combinations that will be supported, and those that will not be implemented, based on the requirements for your web service.

Note that besides POST, PUT, GET and DELETE, there are a few more HTTP methods, including HEAD which retrieve metadata for a resource identified by a URI. It is useful, for example, to know that HEAD can be used to retrieve a resource's version. We will not use it in our web service examples, however.

Let's try to create a table listing all the methods we may wish to support in the MTA web service:

```
URL             Method   Supported   Description
/orders         GET      yes         retrieve a list of orders
/orders         POST     yes         add a new order
/orders         PUT      no          update entire collection
/orders         DELETE   no          delete entire collection

/orders/<id>    GET      yes         get order with ID <id>
/orders/<id>    POST     no          add an order to existing order <id>
/orders/<id>    PUT      yes         update order with ID <id>
/orders/<id>    DELETE   yes         delete order with ID <id>
```

A table such as this is a useful piece of information for consumers of our API. It can even be built according to the methods being allowed per API consumer. For example, it could consist of a list of operations allowed on orders linked to the customer consuming our web service. We will try to semi-automatically build such a table in Chapter 12.

If we want to consume the REST service ourselves, and retrieve order information for a specific costumer, more parameters might be involved, resulting in slightly more complex URIs:

```
URL                       Method   Supported   Description
/cust/<cid>/orders        GET      yes         get orders for customer
/cust/<cid>/orders        POST     yes         add a new order
/cust/<cid>/orders        PUT      yes         update entire list
/cust/<cid>/orders        DELETE   yes         delete entire list

/cust/<cid>/orders/<id>   GET      yes         get a specific order
/cust/<cid>/orders/<id>   POST     no          add an order to order <id>
/cust/<cid>/orders/<id>   PUT      yes         update order <id>
/cust/<cid>/orders/<id>   DELETE   yes         delete order <id>
```

How we map these URIs and methods to actual code and data being returned will become clearer in the examples further on.

We can add to the information in these tables by listing the possible response and error codes. A few useful HTTP response codes are listed here:

```
200     OK                      Request was successful
201     Created                 The object or resource is created
400     Bad Request             Request is not understood or was malformed. An
    explanation may be available in the body of the response
403     Forbidden               Permission denied or authentication
    credentials invalid
404     Not Found               Resource could not be found
405     Method Not Allowed      The action (POST, PUT, ...) is not allowed on
    the resource
410     Gone                    Resource no longer exists
500     Internal Server Error   Something went wrong on the server side
501     Not Implemented         The action is not available
```

Since REST is not a protocol or standard, you are not technically obliged to use these response codes. Most REST clients expect them, however, and since REST and HTTP are closely related, using these well-known HTTP response codes is certainly the best solution. Also, most developers working with your REST service are likely to be already familiar with at least a few of them.

A web service or application following the REST philosophy is described as being RESTful. The term REST was originally coined by Roy Fielding, one of the authors of the HTTP specification. In its most basic form, you could consider the web as being partly RESTful. Also note the analogy with the often used term CRUD (Create, Read, Update and Delete) which sums up all of the actions possible when handling an object or record from a database table.

While REST was originally described using XML as structured data, strictly speaking it is payload-agnostic, and in fact JSON is replacing XML as the preferred message format in many cases. You can build powerful applications using JSON-based REST in combination with JavaScript and AJAX interfaces, since many JavaScript libraries such as jQuery have good support for REST calls. By way of further example, the document-oriented database CouchDB uses REST for communication and JSON for data storage and message passing.

As we will see, using PHP and Zend Framework we can easily return JSON and other data types upon request: XML, JSON, serialized PHP arrays and objects or even binary-encoded XML. In our examples we will have a look at optionally returning other types of data.

Worth mentioning is that some firewalls block PUT and DELETE requests, and only allow POST and GET, which should be kept in mind when encountering odd and unexpected results while testing. There are workarounds for this: you could for example allow your REST server to identify a PUT request by accepting:

-a POST request with a _method=PUT parameter attached to the URL -an extra header, X-HTTP-Method-Override: PUT with the POST request

Both could in fact be detected and used by your REST server to identify a POST request as actually being a PUT request in disguise. The same could be done for DELETE requests. Of course, straight PUT requests should be supported alongside both mentioned workarounds too; the above solution only allows for clients encountering problems with PUT and DELETE to fully consume your service.

REST versus POX versus RPC versus Pure REST

The term REST is sometimes used lightly, for example to describe GET calls that return plain XML, without further support for other REST aspects like creating and deleting a resource. An ad hoc GET call to a URI with an RSS feed could be considered RESTful, albeit in a limited sense. A POST call to a URI for placing an order returning XML, and no further methods for retrieving or updating an order, is not RESTful.

What is described above is an example of semi-open URI endpoints often described as POX or Plain Old XML over HTTP, and actually leans more towards SOAP and RPC than REST. There is a lot of business logic assumed to be known by the consumer of the service. While the SOAP/WSDL combination offers you a way of describing that logic, POX is usually only as powerful as the accompanying documentation offered to the service consumer.

The line between these half-baked API interfaces and real RESTful APIs, however, is thin, and at times it attracts quite hefty debate. There are even a number of public and well known web services that tout themselves to be RESTful, while in fact, they are not. So, plenty of room exists for interpretation and discussion.

Note that while RSS is considered only partly RESTful because it only supports GET for retrieving a collection and sometimes individual items from a news feed: Atom, a newer format, consists of two components; the Atom Syndication Format (an XML format used mainly for news feeds) accompanied by the Atom Publishing Protocol, also known as AtomPub or APP. Together they describe not only a way of exposing news feeds, or content in general; but also a means of updating and manipulating them. APP is considered a prime example of a RESTful protocol. Wordpress, for example, has a built-in APP enabled service that allows for AtomPub clients to create, retrieve, update and delete posts and files without using the classic web based admin interface.

Concerning the "SOAP versus" discussion, RESTafarians (or RESTifarians, true REST followers) often argue that SOAP reinvents the wheel, since HTTP already offers many verbs to define different kinds of actions on the resources being represented by URLs. Using SOAP requires you to define and describe each and every exposed operation, like the createOrder() method we saw previously. In fact, SOAP means defining and verbosely describing an entire set of verbs; while using REST means accepting or not accepting a number of actions on a URI. Arguments on both sides of this RPC/SOAP versus REST debate can be found all over the Net. It is up to you to form your own opinion on this, and use the techniques most suited for your situation.

REST and PHP

There is no REST equivalent of `SoapServer` and `SoapClient` in PHP, but the language does provide you with all the tools needed for building a REST server and REST clients. You can build a server yourself using tools like cURL, or `file_get_contents()` with options set for stream wrappers and so on. By doing so, you provide a solution for handling the PUT, POST, GET and DELETE requests.

Let's create a very simple REST server, where we first try to detect which HTTP method or verb we are dealing with:

```
$data = NULL;
$id   = NULL;

switch ($_SERVER['REQUEST_METHOD']) {
    case 'GET':
        $type = 'GET';
        if (isset($_GET['id'])) {
            $id = $_GET['id'];
        }
```

```
            break;
        case 'POST':
        case 'PUT':
        case 'DELETE':
            $data = file_get_contents('php://input');
            if (isset($_GET['id'])) {
                $id = $_GET['id'];
            }
            $type = $_SERVER['REQUEST_METHOD'];
            if ($_SERVER['REQUEST_METHOD'] == 'POST') {
                if (isset($_GET['_method'])) {
                    switch($_GET['_method']) {
                        case 'PUT':
                        case 'DELETE':
                        case 'POST':
                            $type = $_GET['_method'];
                            break;
                        default:
                            $type = 'UNKNOWN';
                    }
                }
            }
            break;
        default:
            $type = 'UNKNOWN';
            break;
    }
```

Note that we added support for the _method=PUT workaround. The following few lines show how we will handle GET requests for a list of orders or an individual order. For this example, order information is stored as flat text files in a directory.

```
$filedir = '../data/orders/';

switch ($type) {
    case 'GET':
        if (is_numeric($id)) {
            $file = $filedir.(int) $id.'.txt';
            if (file_exists($file)) {
                echo sendResponse(200, file_get_contents($file)); // ok
            } else {
                echo sendResponse(410,''); // gone
            }
        } else {
```

82 ■ REST

```
            $listing = scandir($filedir);
            $list = array();
            foreach ($listing as $file) {
               if ($file !== '.' && $file !== '..') {
                  $list[] = basename($file);
               }
            }
            echo sendResponse(200, $list); // ok
         }
         break;
      case 'POST':
      case 'DELETE':
      case 'PUT':
         echo sendResponse(501,''); // not yet implemented
         break;
   }
```

Handling of the PUT, POST and DELETE methods will be done afterwards; first we want to test our server. The next example shows how we create a response. Response codes are sent in the response header and inside the XML payload:

```
   function sendResponse($status, $payload)
   {
      $respcodes = array( 200 => 'OK',
                          201 => 'Created',
                          204 => 'No Content',
                          301 => 'Moved permanently',
                          400 => 'Bad Request',
                          404 => 'Not found',
                          410 => 'Gone',
                          501 => 'Not implemented'
                        );
      header('HTTP/1.1 ' . $status . ' ' . $respcodes[$status]);
      header('Content-type: text/xml');
      $xml = '<?xml version="1.0" encoding="UTF-8"?>';
      $xml .= '<response>';
      $xml .= '<code>' . $status . '</ code>';
      $xml .= '<message>' . $respcodes[$status] . '</message>';
      if (!empty($payload)) {
         $xml .= '<data>';
         if (is_array($payload)) {
            foreach ($payload as $item) {
               $xml .= '<item>' . (string) $item . '</item>';
            }
```

```
        } else {
            $xml .= (string) $payload;
        }
        $xml .= '</data>';
    }
    $xml .= '</response>';
    echo $xml;
}
```

Many more response codes could be implemented of course, as we are only using a small set in our example here. Our REST server reads, stores, and deletes order information in text files inside the data directory. In real life, and in later examples, we will be using the database as our back end.

In our example we only listen for requests issued against orders. Some extra work would be needed in order to support exposure of additional resources like invoices. Incoming calls could be mapped to their corresponding handlers, for example. You could do some URL rewriting based on HTTP conditions to facilitate incoming requests being sent to the correct handler or you could build a list of URLs and map them using regular expressions to the correct handler.

So much for the server: Creating requests against a REST web service is actually quite easy too. You can simply issue a GET call and fetch information from a remote service by using file_get_contents(), and parsing the incoming XML using DOM, XMLReader or SimpleXML.

Now let us test our own example REST server:

```
$xmlstring = file_get_contents('http://zfws/restserver.php');
$xmlobj = simplexml_load_string($xmlstring);
echo '<pre>' . htmlentities($xmlobj->asXML()) . '</pre>'; // for debugging
```

This performs a GET call to the URL of our REST server and retrieves a list of orders. The output is loaded as a SimpleXMLElement object. From this point on you can parse and handle the data contained inside the XML message. If opening remote files is disallowed in PHP's configuration (via the allow_url_fopen php.ini setting) as a security measure by your hosting provider for example, you can use the cURL extension to work around this limitation (see Appendix B).

When trying to call a non-existing order, you will receive the HTTP header HTTP/1.1 410 Gone. The request:

```
$xmlstring = file_get_contents('http://zfws/restserver.php?id=-1');
$responseheaders = explode(' ',$http_response_header[0]);
if ($responseheaders['1'] == '200') {
   $xmlobj = simplexml_load_string($xmlstring);
   echo '<pre>'  .htmlentities($xmlobj->asXML()) . '</pre>'; // for debugging
} else {
   echo $http_response_header[0];
}
```

And the resulting XML response:

```
<?xml version="1.0" encoding="UTF-8"?>
<response>
   <code>410</ code>
   <message>Gone</message>
</response>
```

You could have tested that as well by simply pointing your browser at http://zfws/restserver.php?id=-1. In our code, we do not output the resulting XML since file_get_contents() returns false when it encounters an error, in this case a response code other than 200. If you want to have a peek at the above XML, you could use a cURL-based solution, or just open up and use a conventional browser like Firefox. We will have another look at a solution for talking to a REST server in the Zend Framework-based solutions further in this chapter.

PHP's stream wrappers not only support GET, they also allow for using file_get_contents() to send a POST message too. Let's try to create an order, something our REST service will not allow us to do just yet:

```
$options = array(
   'http' => array(
      'method'  => "POST",
      'content' => http_build_query(array('id' => 123))
   )
);

$context   = stream_context_create($options);
$xmlstring = file_get_contents('http://zfws/restserver.php', false, $context);

// The $http_response_header array is automatically populated
// when using the HTTP stream wrapper
```

```
$responseheaders = explode(' ', $http_response_header[0]);
if ($responseheaders['1'] == '200') {
   $xmlobj = simplexml_load_string($xmlstring);
   echo '<pre>' . htmlentities($xmlobj->asXML()) . '</pre>'; // for debugging
} else {
   echo $http_response_header[0]; //prints out '501'
}
```

The resulting response (HTTP/1.1 501 Not Implemented) tells us that use of the POST for creating an order is not yet implemented.

Now, let's quickly add support for POST, PUT and DELETE, resulting in restserver2.php, before finally moving our solution to one based on Zend_Rest:

```
switch ($type) {
   // ...
   case 'POST':
      if (is_numeric($id)) {
         echo sendResponse(501, ''); //not yet implemented
      } else {
         $newid = time();
         $file  = $filedir.'ORDER_'.$newid.'.txt';
         error_reporting(0); // xdebug might spit some output otherwise
                             // resulting in a 200 response header
         $dom = new DOMDocument();
         if (!$dom->loadXML((string) $data)) {
            echo sendResponse(400, ''); // Bad request, invalid XML
         } else {
            $xml = simplexml_load_string((string) $data);
            if (isset($xml->data)) {
               file_put_contents($file, (string) $xml->data);
               echo sendResponse(201, '/restserver2.php?id=' . $newid);
               // Created
            } else {
               echo sendResponse(400,''); // Bad request, missing data
            }
         }
      }
      break;
   case 'DELETE':
      if (is_numeric($id)) {
         $file = $filedir . 'ORDER_' . (int) $id . '.txt';
         if (file_exists($file)) {
            unlink($file);
            echo sendResponse(204, ''); // No content (but ok)
```

```
            } else {
                echo sendResponse(404, ''); // Not found
            }
        } else {
            echo sendResponse(501,''); // Not yet implemented
        }
        break;
    case 'PUT':
        if (is_numeric($id)) {
            $file = $filedir . 'ORDER_' . (int) $id . '.txt';
            if (file_exists($file)) {
                $dom = new DOMDocument();
                if(!$dom->loadXML((string) $data)) {
                    echo sendResponse(400, ''); // Bad request, invalid XML
                } else {
                    $xml = simplexml_load_string($data);
                    if (isset($xml->data)) {
                        file_put_contents($file, (string) $xml->data);
                        echo sendResponse(200, file_get_contents($file));
                    } else {
                        echo sendResponse(400, '');// Bad request, missing data
                    }
                }
            } else {
                echo sendResponse(404, '');//Not found
            }
        } else {
            echo sendResponse(501, ''); // Not yet implemented
        }
        break;
    // ...
}
```

The POST handler accepts input and creates an order file in our data/orders/ directory. An example call creating an order could look like so:

```
$msg = 'New order info submitted at '.date('Ymd H:i:s');
$xml = '<?xml version="1.0" encoding="UTF-8"?>';
$xml .= '<request>';
$xml .= '<data>'.$msg.'</data>';
$xml .= '</request>';

$options = array(
    'http' => array(
        'method'  => "POST",
```

```
        'content '=> $xml
    )
);

$context   = stream_context_create($options);
$xmlstring = file_get_contents('http://zfws/restserver2.php', false, $context);
```

This will result in a new file named data/orders/ORDER_<new order id>.txt. Note that you could also send an additional header alongside the response body:

```
Location: /restserver2.php?id=<newid>
```

Some clients might choose to follow that URL, while others would pick up the new resource's location from the XML response body. You can choose to offer both, however always be prepared for some critics telling you how un-RESTful or fantastically RESTful your approach is (or is not).

Updating an existing order, for example our already available order "1", could be performed as follows:

```
$msg = 'New info for order 1 submitted at ' . date('Ymd H:i:s');

$xml  = '<?xml version="1.0" encoding="UTF-8"?>';
$xml .= '<request>';
$xml .= '<data>' . $msg . '</data>';
$xml .= '</request>';

$options = array(
    'http' => array(
        'method'  => "PUT",
        'content' => $xml
    )
);

$context   = stream_context_create($options);
$xmlstring = file_get_contents('http://zfws/restserver2.php', false, $context);
```

If you check the content of the order, you will see that it is updated by the REST service. The same could be done for deleting an order, sending DELETE as the method and an empty body. In production code, all this should be nicely wrapped inside functions or request and response objects of course, while handling errors and abstracting away all those low-level calls.

To conclude, you must keep two things in mind when creating a REST server yourself: First, it will require some work to do all this using custom code, but it is possible. Second, response and error codes are vital when dealing with REST. This applies on the client side as well as on the server side, so you should be very careful to handle all possible error and response codes that you know to be used by the server. Documentation accompanying the web service can guide you on these.

Creating the REST Service Using Zend Framework

Zend Framework has a `Zend_Rest` component that provides us with both server and client functionality. The server part follows the same flow as does the SOAP server. You instantiate a REST server and assign some functions or a class to which the incoming requests will be passed. You cannot assign an object however.

In its most basic form, you could create a REST server like this:

```
Zend_Loader::loadClass('Mta_Service');
$server = new Zend_Rest_Server();
$server->setClass('Mta_Service');
$server->handle();
```

If you save this as `REST.php` and browse to the corresponding URL (`http://zfws/REST.php`), you'll see something like this:

```
<?xml version="1.0" encoding="UTF-8"?>
<rest generator="zend" version="1.0">
   <response>
      <message>No Method Specified.</message>
   </response>
   <status>failed</status>
</rest>
```

`Zend_Rest_Server` expects the arguments for the class to be given in the URL. Browsing `http://zfws/REST.php?method=getStockFigures&product_id=1` would result in:

```xml
<?xml version="1.0" encoding="UTF-8"?>
<Mta_Service generator="zend" version="1.0">
   <getStockFigures>
      <response>111</response>
      <status>success</status>
   </getStockFigures>
</Mta_Service>
```

If your method returns an XML object generated using SimpleXML or DOM for example, it will return the response unchanged as the result. This gives you an easy way of overriding the XML structures that `Zend_Rest_Server` generates for you.

If you paid attention in previous chapters, you can easily guess how and where `Zend_Rest_Server` gets the necessary information for mapping these requests and responses to the supplied class. It uses reflection and information contained in docblocks, the same information used by `Zend_Soap_Server`.

You could even output some information if no specific method is called:

```php
Zend_Loader::loadClass('Mta_Service');

$server = new Zend_Rest_Server();
$server->setClass('Mta_Service');
if (isset($_GET['__info__'])) {
   header('HTTP/1.1 200 Ok');
   header('Content-type: text/xml');
   $xml = '<?xml version="1.0" encoding="UTF-8"?>';
   $xml .= '<response>';
   $xml .= '<operations>';
   foreach ($server->getFunctions() as $function) {
      $xml .= '<method>' . $function->getName() . '</method>';
   }
   $xml .= '</operations>';
   $xml .= '<code>200</ code>';
   $xml .= '</response>';
   echo $xml;
} else {
   $server->handle();
}
```

Browsing /REST.php?__info__=1 will list all available methods. You could add more info such as required parameters and return value information, since `getFunctions()` returns an array with reflection objects loaded with info for each method.

Querying the web service is convenient too, using `Zend_Rest_Client`:

```
require_once('Zend/Loader.php');
Zend_Loader::loadClass('Zend_Rest_Client');
$client = new Zend_Rest_Client('http://zfws/REST.php');
$result = $client->getStockFigures(1)->get();
if ($result->isSuccess()) {
    echo $result;
}
```

This will result in the stock total for the product being displayed.

All in all, this is a nice and convenient solution, but where is the concept of resources? This does not seem to be resource oriented at all, but rather an RPC-like style of exposing XML through playing with URL parameters. Is this approach RESTful anyway? Let us explore it a bit further before going into more detail on this.

For example, how are we going to handle POST, PUT and DELETE? How do we hook these easily into `Zend_Rest_Server`? You could add some code to a controller action, add some detection of whether the request is a POST, PUT, DELETE or a GET HTTP method and act accordingly. For example:

```
class RestController extends Zend_Controller_Action
{
    public function init()
    {
        $this->_server = Zend_Loader::loadClass('Mta_Service');
        $server = new Zend_Rest_Server();
        $server->setClass('Mta_Service');
    }

    public function orderAction()
    {
        $this->_helper->viewRenderer->setNoRender(); // no view involved

        // do the checks for order ID, GET, POST and so on and
        // act as expected
        // ...
        $request = array();

        $id = $this->_request->getParam('order_id');
```

```
        if ($this->_request->isGet()) {
            if (isset($id) && is_numeric($id) {
                $request['method'] = 'getOrder';
                $request['params'] = array('order_id' => $id);

            } else {
                $request['method'] = 'getOrders';
                $request['params'] = array(); // eventually customerid here
            }
            $server->handle($request);
        } elseif ($this->_request->isPost()) {
            $xmlstring = $this->_request->getRawBody();
            $xml = simplexml_load_string($xmlstring);
            // ...
        }
        // ... and so on ...
    }
}
```

The request array is created, the class method to be used is specified and the requested ID is taken from the GET string. The resulting request array is handed over to the server instance. If no order ID is found in the URL, the full list of orders could be returned. This approach also implies that for each exposed resource we have to create an action method in the controller, containing code to detect GET, POST and so on, using the isGet(), isPut(), isDelete() and isPost() methods of the request object. As you can see, a lot of tedious and repetitive coding is involved in this code example. Preparing the request before handing it over to the server as shown above is reminiscent of the preprocessing we explored in the SOAP chapter.

So the Zend_Rest_Server solution described so far does offer some ease of adding methods as the endpoints for the REST server methods. Handling each call by hand-coding every little piece as we did above does not offer much advantage over custom-created PHP code. You basically map and categorize each incoming call, and hand it over to the correct method of the class set for powering the REST server.

A more important point of concern is that Zend_Rest_Server exposes methods of a class that is assigned for handling the calls. You read that correctly: *methods* and not *resources*. It is a wrapper for conveniently creating an XML response for each method being talked to, but not an out-of-the-box solution for exposing resources. Furthermore, the requirement to encode messages in XML means that Zend_Rest is not payload-agnostic. In fact, it is more of an RPC-style approach than a RESTful solution. That is the main reason Zend_Rest_Server will be deprecated in future versions of Zend Framework. Since it will still be there for the time being, and references to it are still found in the Zend Framework manual and on the internet, we had to have a brief look at it.

Zend_Rest_Client will stay for a while, but you can also use Zend_Http_Client to talk to remote REST servers, and so we will have a look at the latter in due course.

The preferred approach now offered by Zend Framework's REST support, since version 1.9, is a combination of Zend_Rest_Controller and Zend_Rest_Route.

Zend_Rest_Route

Routing in Zend Framework is mostly performed by the standard router, Zend_Controller_Router_Rewrite, which makes sure that URLs are mapped to the correct module, controller and action.

A browser pointed to /orders/archive/print/id/1 will result in calling printAction() in the Order_ArchiveController inside the "orders" module, making "id" available as a request parameter, in this case initialized to "1". Zend Framework allows for customizing the router's behavior, however. For example, you may want to drop the "id" from the URL and add a route like this one in the Bootstrap.php file:

```
protected function _initExampleRoute()
{
   $this->bootstrap('frontController');
   $frontController = Zend_Controller_Front::getInstance();
   $router = $frontController->getRouter();
   $route = new Zend_Controller_Router_Route(
            '/archive/print/:id',
            array(
               'module'     => 'default',
               'controller' => 'index',
               'action'     => 'index'
            ),
            array('id' => '\d+')
         );
   $router->addRoute('test', $route);
}
```

Methods starting with _init are picked up by the bootstrapping process. Now a call to /orders/archive/print/1 will result in the same output as the one produced with the above URI. Every imaginable virtual routing can be done using Zend Framework's routing tools. You can for example add routes using regular expressions, by defining and adding a Zend_Controller_Router_Route_Regex-based route. Even better, route configurations can be stored in a Zend_Config object (and therefore stored in an XML or INI file) and that object can be assigned to the router too. This allows for multiple routes being defined in a consistent and legible manner.

The recently added Zend_Rest_Route allows for assigning REST-based routes to modules, certain controllers, certain actions or even the entire application. In the latter case, if it is the default route, all controllers will be considered REST controllers. Adding a REST-specific route is as simple as adding a normal route. You can instantiate Zend_Rest_Route in the application Bootstrap.php file like this:

```
protected function _initRestroutes()
{
    $this->bootstrap('frontController');
    $frontController = Zend_Controller_Front::getInstance();
    $restRoute = new Zend_Rest_Route($frontController, array(), array('rest'))
        ;
    $frontController->getRouter()->addRoute('restroute', $restRoute);
}
```

This will result in all controllers residing in the module named "rest" being considered as REST controllers. You can do the same for the "default" module, resulting in the entire application being considered restful, or just for a few controllers.

If you were to choose to assign only one controller as RESTful, you could do something similar to this:

```
$restRoute = new Zend_Rest_Route($frontController, array(), array(
    'admin' => array('user'),
));
$frontController->getRouter()->addRoute('adminrestroute', $restRoute);
```

This would result in the Admin_UserController() being treated as RESTful.

What is particularly special about Zend_Rest_Route is that it will not only rewrite URL parts, but will also detect HTTP verbs like POST, and send the request to a predefined list of corresponding actions. The first example, which specified that the entire module named "rest" should be considered RESTful, will result in behavior like this:

	URI	Module_Controller	Action
GET	/rest/products/	Rest_ProductsController	indexAction()
GET	/rest/products/:id	Rest_ProductsController	getAction()
POST	/rest/products	Rest_ProductsController	postAction()
PUT	/rest/products/:id	Rest_ProductsController	putAction()
DELETE	/rest/products/:id	Rest_ProductsController	deleteAction()

These additional URL formats are supported too, as a workaround for environments where PUT or DELETE are not supported, for example if they are blocked by a firewall:

	URI	Module_Controller	Action
POST	/rest/products/:id?_method=PUT	Rest_ProductsController	putAction()
POST	/rest/products/:id?_method=DELETE	Rest_ProductsController	deleteAction()

This applies for every controller in the module named "rest", as they are all considered RESTful.

Zend_Rest_Controller

How do you create a controller that receives all these REST requests as directed by the Zend_Rest_Route configuration? Simple, you extend Zend_Rest_Controller. This is an abstract class specifying these abstract methods; the following comes straight from the Zend Framework source code:

```
abstract class Zend_Rest_Controller extends Zend_Controller_Action
{
   /**
    * The index action handles index/list requests; it should respond with a
    * list of the requested resources.
    */
   abstract public function indexAction();

   /**
    * The get action handles GET requests and receives an 'id' parameter; it
    * should respond with the server resource state of the resource identified
```

```
     * by the 'id' value.
     */
    abstract public function getAction();

    /**
     * The post action handles POST requests; it should accept and digest a
     * POSTed resource representation and persist the resource state.
     */
    abstract public function postAction();

    /**
     * The put action handles PUT requests and receives an 'id' parameter; it
     * should update the server resource state of the resource identified by
     * the 'id' value.
     */
    abstract public function putAction();

    /**
     * The delete action handles DELETE requests and receives an 'id'
     * parameter; it should update the server resource state of the resource
     * identified by the 'id' value.
     */
    abstract public function deleteAction();
}
```

The comments explain things nicely. This class provides guidelines on how to implement your own REST controller. Note that you can define these methods without extending from Zend_Rest_Controller, as long as they are there and handle REST requests as expected, everything is fine.

Combined with the routing part, Zend_Rest_Controller gives you plenty of flexibility. We will have a closer look at some more example code later in this chapter and that will further demonstrate this approach.

Zend_Http_Client

You could continue to use Zend_Rest_Client and its semi-magic method calls, or you could choose to use Zend_Http_Client, which gives you more control over the headers and body being sent. Here is a small piece of code that shows you how to use Zend_Http_Client to send an XML string as the body of a POST request:

```
$xml = '<order>';
$xml .= '<data>Product ID 123456</data>';
$xml .= '</order>';
$client = new Zend_Http_Client('http://zfws/restserver2.php');
$response = $client->setRawData($xml, 'text/xml')->request('POST');
```

That is a call comparable to the Zend_Rest_Client-based one we saw previously. The next listing shows what the resulting Zend_Http_Response object looks like:

```
Zend_Http_Response Object
(
    [version:protected] => 1.1
    [code:protected] => 201
    [message:protected] => Created
    [headers:protected] => Array
        (
            [Date] => Wed, 1 Apr 2010 19:55:07 GMT
            [Server] => Apache/2.2.12 (Ubuntu)
            [X-powered-by] => PHP/5.2.10-2ubuntu6.4
            [Vary] => Accept-Encoding
            [Content-encoding] => gzip
            [Content-length] => 137
            [Connection] => close
            [Content-type] => text/xml
        )

    [body:protected] => ...Gzip compressed data....
)
```

Zend_Http_Client negotiated the Gzip compression with the server using the detected HTTP headers, and gives us a Zend_Http_Response object as a result, which in turn gives us access to the headers, response code, response message, content and even the raw content, using the public methods getHeaders(), getStatus(), getMessage(), getBody() and getRawBody().

Zend_Http_Client also allows for defining authentication headers, alongside all other kinds of request headers, and can be used as another alternative for plain cURL- or file_get_contents()-based solutions.

Something not previously mentioned, in case you wonder how it is done: Zend Framework handles PUT requests by parsing the incoming request body and making the parts available as request parameters, just like the GET and POST parameters. This is done inside Zend_Controller_Plugin_PutHandler.

Some Example Code

Let us first create our own controller class to extend from:

```
class Mta_Rest_Controller extends Zend_Rest_Controller
{
   public function init()
   {
      if (Zend_Controller_Action_HelperBroker::hasHelper('layout')) {
         $this->_helper->layout->disableLayout();
      }
      $this->_helper->viewRenderer->setNoRender(true);

      // set the response code
      $this->_response->setHttpResponseCode(501);

      // create an instance of our response object
      $this->_output = new Mta_Rest_Response();

      // set code for the output/response object
      $this->_output->setCode(501);

      // set the body of the output/response object
      $this->_output->setBody('Method Not Implemented');
   }

   public function indexAction()
   {
      $this->_response->setHeader('content-type',
                                  $this->_output->getType(),
                                  true);
      $this->_response->setBody($this->_output->getOutput());
   }

   // ... repeat code of last method for putAction(), getAction(), ...
}
```

What is happening here? First we disable Zend_Layout if it is available, followed by turning off the rendering of view scripts. By default we return a 501 response code ("Not implemented") for this base REST controller. For each HTTP verb we create a method that sets the response header ("501 Not Implemented" by default) and the response body.

Our responses are created by an object instantiated from `Mta_Rest_Response`. This class prepares the XML or JSON response code and message body and these values are assigned inside `indexAction()`, `putAction()` and so on as the actual framework response parts.

`Mta_Rest_Response` is as follows:

```php
class Mta_Rest_Response
{
    private $_code  = 200;
    private $_body  = NULL;
    private $_type  = 'xml';
    private $_json  = NULL;
    private $_xml   = NULL;
    private $_ctype = 'application/xml';

    public function __construct($options = array())
    {
      // ... some options can be set using __construct too ...
    }

    public function setType($type = 'xml')
    {
       if (in_array($type,array('xml','json'))) {
          $this->_type = $type;
          switch($type) {
             case 'xml':
             default:
                $this->_ctype = 'application/xml';
                break;
             case 'json':
                $this->_ctype = 'application/json';
                break;
          }
       }
    }

    public function getType()
    {
        return $this->_type;
    }
```

```
public function setCode($code = 200)
{
   $this->_code = $code;
}

public function getCode()
{
   return $this->_code;
}

public function setBody($data = NULL)
{
   $body = NULL;
   if ($data instanceof Zend_Db_Table_Rowset) {
      $data = $data->toArray();
      $cnt = 0;
      foreach ($data as $row) {
         $body[$cnt] = array();
         $body[$cnt] = array();
         foreach ($row as $column => $value) {
            $body[$cnt][$column] = $value;
         }
         $cnt++;
      }
   }
   $this->_body = $body;
}

public function getBody()
{
   return $this->_body;
}

public function getXml()
{
   $xml = '<response>';
   $xml .= '<code>' . $this->_code . '</ code>';
   if (is_string($this->_body)) {
      $xml .= '<msg>' . $this->_body . '</msg>';
   } elseif (is_array($this->_body)) {
      $xml .= '<msg>';
      foreach ($this->_body as $items) {
         $xml .= '<item>';
         foreach ($items as $key => $val) {
            $xml .= "<$key>$val</$key>";
         }
```

```
            $xml .= '</item>';
        }
        $xml .= '</msg>';
    }
    $xml .= '</response>';
    $this->_xml = simplexml_load_string($xml);
    return $this->_xml->asXML();
}

public function getJson()
{
    $this->_json = new stdClass();
    $this->_json->code = $this->_code;
    $this->_json->body = $this->_body;
    return Zend_Json::encode($this->_json);
}

public function getOutput($type = NULL)
{
    if (!is_null($type)) {
        $this->setType($type);
    }
    switch($this->_type) {
       case 'json':
           return $this->getJson();
           break;
       case 'xml':
       default:
           return $this->getXml();
           break;
    }
}

public function getCtype()
{
    return $this->_ctype;
}
}
```

The class allows for setting a few private properties such as the response code, the body holding the eventual information of the response being created, and a response type. Indeed, as an alternative to XML we would like our response to be sent as JSON, if the client supports it. For now, our base REST controller class creates the response object using XML as the type, but we will add JSON shortly.

Note that you could also use `Zend_Controller_Action_Helper_ContextSwitch` to allow for detecting supported response types. That helper uses different views for different output types, but I prefer not to use it for our examples. The approach seems more suitable for Ajax response handling. You can take a look at the manual[1] for more information.

What is the point of adding another REST controller class to extend from? This allows us, for example, to have a generic error ready for every REST request directed at the actual controllers. Suppose you start to develop your actual REST controller that will talk and expose a Product resource like so:

```
class Rest_ProductsController extends Mta_Rest_Controller
{
    // ...
}
```

This controller is placed in the "rest" module which we declared RESTful using `Zend_Rest_Route`, and should be able to handle all kinds of REST requests, although as you can see, it bears no code so far.

Firing a request at it can be achieved like so:

```
$client = new Zend_Http_Client('http://zfws/rest/products/1');
$response = $client->request();
echo $response->getMessage();
```

This will show you "Method Not Implemented". This tells us that your controller is listening and responding in a RESTful way. This is not inherently very useful, but you can now start adding code to talk to the `Mta_Model_Product` model and the product-related tables in the database to create some more meaningful responses.

Let's add the option to retrieve a list of products:

```
class Rest_OrdersController extends Mta_Rest_Controller
{
    public function indexAction()
    {
        $order = new Mta_Model_Order();
        $result = $order->fetchAll();
```

---

[1] http://framework.zend.com/manual/1.0/en/zend.controller.actionhelpers.html

```
        $this->_output->setCode(200);
        $this->_output->setBody($result);

        $this->_response->setHttpResponseCode(200);
        $this->_response->setHeader('content-type',
                                    $this->_output->getType(),
                                    true);
        $this->_response->setBody($this->_output->getOutput());
    }
}
```

The special init() method in the parent controller class is called automatically by the Zend Framework dispatch flow, and this creates a default response object named $_output, based on Mta_Rest_Response. We fetch all orders and pass "200" as the desired response code and the result to the $_output object.

Next, Zend Framework's response object is manipulated by setting the HTTP status code to "200", the Content-Type header to "application/xml", and the XML string created by $_output as the body.

The resulting response is fetched like so:

```
$client = new Zend_Http_Client('http://zfws/rest/orders/');
$response = $client->request();
echo $response->getBody();
```

This response looks like the following XML structure:

```
<?xml version="1.0"?>
<response>
   <code>200</ code>
   <msg>
      <item>
         <order_id>1</order_id>
         <order_customer_id>1</order_customer_id>
      </item>
      <item>
         <order_id>2</order_id>
         <order_customer_id>2</order_customer_id>
      </item>
   </msg>
</response>
```

In `Mta_Rest_Response`, the `setBody()` method detects a `Zend_Db_Table_Rowset` object as data being passed, and turns it into an associative array ready for generating the XML response. You could add detection of multiple types of data being handed over to `setBody()` and prepare the data as suited.

Suppose you want to add support for JSON. We already have a `getJson()` method in `Mta_Rest_Response`, but how can we see what types of responses the client supports? In `Mta_Rest_Controller`, you could pass the "`Accept`" header as sent by the client querying your REST service:

```
class Mta_Rest_Controller extends Zend_Rest_Controller
{
    public function init()
    {
        // ...

        //pass the Accept headers
        $this->_output->setAcceptheaders($this->_request->getHeader('Accept'));

        // ...
    }
}
```

This will pass a comma-separated string of the known and supported response types which the REST client (a browser, a JavaScript library or an HTTP aware piece of code) accepts.

In `Mta_Rest_Response` we add two more methods:

```
// ...

public function setAcceptheaders($headerstring = '')
{
    $this->_acceptheaders = explode(',', $headerstring);
}

public function setType($type = 'auto')
{
    if ($type == 'auto' && $this->_acceptheaders) {
        if (in_array('application/json', $this->_acceptheaders)) {
            $type = 'json';
        } elseif (in_array('application/xml', $this->_acceptheaders)) {
            $type = 'xml';
```

```
            }
        }
        if (in_array($type,array('xml', 'json'))) {
            $this->_type = $type;
            switch($type) {
                case 'xml':
                default:
                    $this->_ctype = 'application/xml';
                    break;
                case 'json':
                    $this->_ctype = 'application/json';
                    break;
            }
        }
    }
```

Now, the output type is being detected and JSON is returned if we try this request:

```
$client = new Zend_Http_Client('http://zfws/rest/orders/');
$client->setHeaders('Accept', 'application/json');
$response = $client->request();
echo $response->getBody();
```

One last thing that we could improve is that we now have a considerable amount of code inside `Rest_OrdersController::indexAction()` that should be reused in all other methods handling PUT, POST, GET and so on. We may be better off placing this code as an additional method inside `Mta_Rest_Controller`:

```
protected function _createResponse($code, $body, $type = 'auto')
{
    $this->_response->setHttpResponseCode($code);
    $this->_output->setCode($code);
    $this->_output->setBody($body);

    $this->_response->setHeader('content-type',
                                $this->_output->getType(),
                                true);
    $this->_response->setBody($this->_output->getOutput($type));
}
```

The resulting `Rest_OrdersController::indexAction()` will look much simpler:

```
public function indexAction()
{
    $order  = new Mta_Model_Order();
    $result = $order->fetchAll();
    $this->_createResponse(200,$result);
}
```

Please note that this could be achieved by creating an action helper too, extending `Zend_Controller_Action_Helper_Abstract`.

Customize the REST Service

We now have a basic working REST web service. Admittedly, some code still needs to be added to handle incoming PUT, POST and DELETE requests, but since they will be routed towards the corresponding actions inside the newly created controllers, it should be fairly easy to do this yourself, based on the examples we saw at the beginning of this chapter. A short example follows:

```
class Rest_OrdersController extends Mta_Rest_Controller
{
    public function getAction()
    {
        $order = new Mta_Model_Order();
        $result = $order->find($this->_request->id);

        if ($result && $result->count()) {
            $this->_createResponse(200, $result);
        } else {
            $this->_createResponse(410, 'Gone');
        }
    }
}
```

This will allow the retrieval of detailed data for a given order. Creating an order should be equally simple:

```
class Rest_CustomersController extends Mta_Rest_Controller
{
    public function indexAction()
```

```php
    {
        $customer = new Mta_Model_Customer();
        $result   = $customer->fetchAll();
        $this->_createResponse(200, $result);
    }

    public function postAction()
    {
        $data = file_get_contents('php://input');
        $dom  = new DOMDocument();
        if (!$dom->loadXML((string) $data)) {
            $this->_createResponse(400);
        } else {
            $xml = simplexml_load_string((string) $data);
            if (isset($xml->data)) {
                $customer = new Mta_Model_Customer();
                $array['customer_name']    = $xml->data->name;
                $array['customer_address'] = $xml->data->address;
                $array['customer_zip']     = $xml->data->zip;
                $array['customer_email']   = $xml->data->email;
                $newid = $customer->insert($array);
                $this->_createResponse(201, '/rest/customer/' . $newid);
            } else {
                $this->_createResponse(400);
            }
        }
    }
}
```

Of course you should do some input validation before just throwing everything to the `Zend_Db_Table` object, but the above was designed only to show you how easy it is to add support for every type of action on the resources.

You might consider moving the handling of incoming data and detection of which type it is (XML or JSON) to the `Mta_Rest_Controller::init()` method. This would be a good thing in terms of code reuse.

Let us revisit some of the custom modifications we did for the SOAP server.

API Version in the URL

Remember that we wanted to add version parameters for our API, in case future backward-incompatible changes would be introduced? How can we achieve this for our REST-based solution? One solution would be to simply add other routes in the Bootstrap.php file, but at the time of writing there is an outstanding bug[2] that mentions issues with Zend_Rest_Route in combination with other routes. A suggested workaround for that issue mentions extending Zend_Rest_Route as a solution and adding custom code for detecting version numbers in the URI.

Suppose you want calls to http://zfws/rest/ and http://zfws/rest/1.0/ to map to our 1.0 version in application/modules/rest/ and calls to http://zfws/rest/2.0/ to map to a different module. It is possible to achieve that using the following workaround:

```
class Mta_Rest_Route extends Zend_Rest_Route
{
   public function match($path, $partial = false)
   {
      $uri = $path->getRequestUri();
      $parts = explode('/',$uri);
      if ($parts['1'] == 'rest' && isset($parts['2'])) {
         if (preg_match('/([0-9]+[.])+([0-9]+)/', $parts['2'])) {
            $version = $parts['2'];
            unset($parts['2']);
            $parts = array_values($parts);
            $uri = implode('/', $parts);

            $front = Zend_Controller_Front::getInstance();
            $front->setControllerDirectory(
                  array(
                     'default' => APPLICATION_PATH . '/controllers',
                     'rest' =>
                      APPLICATION_PATH . '/modules/rest/controllers/' . $version
                      )
                  , 'rest');
         }

         $path->setRequestUri($uri);
         $path->setPathInfo($uri);
      }

      return parent::match($path, $partial);
   }
}
```

[2] http://framework.zend.com/issues/browse/ZF-9372

This solution is based on the ideas posted by Joseph Crawford (who submitted ZF-9372) and the posters who commented on his blog post[3].

What happens inside the custom router class is this: we first extend `Zend_Rest_Route` and parse the URI ourselves before handing it to the `parent::match()` method. We detect whether a version such as 1.0, 2.0, 1.1 etc. is found using `preg_match()`, and move the detected URL parameters so that they correspond with what `Zend_Rest_Route` expects. In case we find a version number specified, we also modify the directory that the controller class should be loaded from. This way, we can have for example a "2.0/" directory inside `application/modules/rest/controllers/`.

The above code now supports URLs like these:

- /rest/orders

- /rest/orders/1

- /rest/2.0/orders

- /rest/2.0/orders/1

By the way, do not forget to modify `Bootstrap.php` to make sure we are using the new router class:

```
protected function _initRestroutes()
{
   $this->bootstrap('frontController');
   $frontController = Zend_Controller_Front::getInstance();

   $router = $frontController->getRouter();
   $restRoute = new Mta_Rest_Route($frontController, array(), array('rest'));
   $router->addRoute('rest', $restRoute);
}
```

Future Zend Framework versions may supply additional ways of adding a version number or adding other additional parameters to the request URI, but we will have to stick with workaround code like the above for the time being.

---

[3] http://www.josephcrawford.com/2010/03/08/zf-creating-restful-applications/

API Key and Preprocessing

API keys can be checked for and accepted in three ways:

- if submitted inside headers as sent by REST clients
- if given as an URL parameter
- if found inside incoming JSON or XML coming from REST client calls

We could build upon the solution offered for adding the API version in the REST URLs. Let's add these lines of code to `Mta_Rest_Route`:

```
class Mta_Rest_Route extends Zend_Rest_Route
{
   public function match($path, $partial = false)
   {
      $uri = $path->getRequestUri();
      $parts = explode('/',$uri);
      if ($parts['1'] == 'rest' && isset($parts['2'])) {
         if (preg_match('/([0-9]+[.])+([0-9]+)/', $parts['2'])) {
            // ... version found and alternate controller dir set ...
         }

         // here we add support for /rest/2.0/orders/apikey/12345
         // and   /rest/orders/apikey/12345
         if (isset($parts[3])) {
            $cnt = 0;
            $newparts = array();
            if (!is_numeric($parts[3])) {
               while ($cnt < 3) {
                  $newparts[] = array_shift($parts);
                  $cnt++;
               }
            } else { // we maintain support for 'id'
               while ($cnt < 4) {
                  $newparts[] = array_shift($parts);
                  $cnt++;
               }
            }
            $uri = implode('/', $newparts);
            $additional = $parts;
         } else {
            $uri = implode('/', $parts);
```

```
                $additional = false;
            }

            $path->setRequestUri($uri);
            $path->setPathInfo($uri);
        }

        $result = parent::match($path, $partial);

        // after we let Zend_Rest_Route do its job, we set the additional
        // parameters like apikey detected above
        if ($additional && is_array($additional)) {
            $key = true;
            for ($i = 0; $i < count($additional); $i++) {
               if ($i%2 == 0) {
                  $result[$additional[$i]] = $additional[$i + 1];
               }
            }
        }
        return $result;
    }
}
```

This removes all parameters not understood by Zend_Rest_Route, handing the result over to Zend_Rest_Route, to let it go through its detection of HTTP verbs, for example. After that, we add the remainder of the URL to the result array and return that extended result array as the new routing match, including the additional parameters.

A call to /rest/orders/apikey/123456 and /rest/2.0/orders/apikey/123456 will result in output as expected. Now we only have to add a check in Mta_Rest_Controller to see if the API key used in the call has access to the methods and resources being requested. You can add a few lines in the init() method, and allow only valid API keys (in this case a hard-coded API key with a value of "654321", purely for the sake of the example):

```
class Mta_Rest_Controller extends Zend_Rest_Controller
{
   public function init()
   {
      // ...

      if ($this->_request->apikey) {
         $contr = $this->_request->getControllerName();
```

```
            $action = $this->_request->getActionName();
            if (!$this->_hasAccess($this->_request->apikey, $contr, $action)) {
                $this->_output->setCode(403);
                $this->_output->setBody('Access denied');
                header("HTTP/1.0 403 Access denied");
                header('content-type: ' . $this->_output->getType());
                echo $this->_output->getOutput();
                exit;
            }
        }
    }

    protected function _hasAccess($apikey, $resource, $action)
    {
        if ((string) $apikey == '654321') {
            return true;
        }
        return false;
    }
}
```

We are now allowing access to all methods only if an API key is found with the value "654321". We will see in Chapter 8 how we can use something more meaningful to apply ACL checks using these API keys.

A call to `http://zfws/rest/orders/apikey/654321` will result in:

```
<?xml version="1.0"?>
<response>
   <code>403</code>
   <msg>Access denied</msg>
</response>
```

Other manipulation and checking of incoming requests can be easily added to the `Mta_Rest_Controller`. Inside the `init()` method we could for example add some code to test for numbers of requests coming from a source IP and disallow too many calls from the same source if necessary, like we did in the SOAP examples.

Summary

- We know what REST means and how to create REST services using Zend Framework

- We were able to add some customizations to our REST service, analogous to the customization done for the SOAP solution

Deliverables:

- We created a REST interface next to the SOAP API. It is almost finished and can accept API keys for each request

Chapter 6

XML-RPC

Introduction

After a healthy dose of REST, we return to a Remote Procedure Call (RPC) approach. XML-RPC[1] is a specification describing how to make procedure calls over the Internet, typically using HTTP or HTTPS for transport, and XML for encoding the payload data. It is considered a predecessor to SOAP.

XML-RPC is similar to, and more formalized than, POX, but not as formalized as SOAP. It supports only a limited set of datatypes and does not have anything like WSDL for SOAP that could allow for more complex datatypes. While clearly an older technology, it still holds ground in many areas, probably because it is so straightforward. For example, XML-RPC is still used in the API of popular blogging platforms like Wordpress and Drupal, to name but two famous examples. Therefore, we should dedicate a least a few pages to it.

The use of XML-RPC implies that a few rules have to be followed, as defined in the XML-RPC specification (often referred to simply as "the spec"). Have a look at this sample XML-RPC request:

```
<?xml version="1.0"?>
<methodCall>
    <methodName>zfws.getStockFigures</methodName>
```

---

[1] http://www.xmlrpc.com/

```
        <params>
            <param>
                <value><int>1</int></value>
            </param>
        </params>
    </methodCall>
```

The XML-RPC spec says:

- The request body is wrapped in a single `<methodCall />` tag
- That container should contain a single `<methodName />` tag
- The method name should be a string only containing a-z, A-Z, 0-9 and any of these characters: _ . : /
- It is entirely up to the server how to interpret this method name
- Parameters for the method being called are contained in a `<params />` element
- Inside the `<params />` element, one or more `<param />` elements are listed
- Each `<param />` tag looks like this: `<param><value>...</value></param>`

The "." notation in the method name allows for the use of namespaces in the calls.

Values for parameters are entered as in the above example, telling the server what type of parameter it is, using an additional tag. Our example sends the parameter as an integer with value "1". If you omit the tag hinting the type, the parameter will be interpreted as a string by default.

As per the spec, these types are supported:

```
Tag                   Type                              Example
<i4> or <int>         32-bit signed integer             -12
<boolean>             0 (false) or 1 (true)             1
<string>              string                            hello
<double>              double-precision signed float     -12.345
<dateTime.iso8601>    date/time                         20100329T08:32:21
<base64>              base64-encoded binary
    eW91IGNhbid0IHJlYWQgdGhpcyE=
```

The <param></params> can be empty. In a string "<" and "&" should be encoded as "<" and "&".

Two more complex data types are available, namely "struct" and "array". A struct is comparable to PHP's associative arrays:

```
<struct>
   <member>
      <name>productname</name>
      <value><string>Wooden bike</string></value>
   </member>
   <member>
      <name>productid</name>
      <value><int>111</int></value>
   </member>
   <member>
      <name>category</name>
      <value><string>Wooden toys</string></value>
   </member>
</struct>
```

An array is comparable to a numbered array in PHP:

```
<array>
   <data>
      <value><string>Wooden toys</string></value>
      <value><string>Electric toys</string></value>
      <value><string>Stuffed toys</string></value>
   </data>
</array>
```

Arrays can contain mixed types. Both arrays and structs can be recursive, so they can contain other arrays or structs. A response looks like this:

```
<?xml version="1.0"?>
<methodResponse>
   <params>
      <param>
         <value>Wooden bike</value>
      </param>
   </params>
</methodResponse>
```

Naturally, responses can contain exactly the same data types as the requests. It is up to the code on the server to check that the appropriate types are being used for input parameters and return values.

Note that there is an extension to the XML-RPC spec[2], adding a `<nil />` value.

In case the server should return an error, it should look like the following XML structure:

```
<?xml version="1.0" encoding="iso-8859-1"?>
<methodResponse>
    <fault>
        <value>
            <struct>
                <member>
                    <name>faultString</name>
                    <value><string>server error. method not found</string></value>
                </member>
                <member>
                    <name>faultCode</name>
                    <value><int>-32601</int></value>
                </member>
            </struct>
        </value>
    </fault>
</methodResponse>
```

So instead of `<params>` we have `<fault>`. Inside the fault tag, we have two members, with the names `faultCode` and `faultString`. The structure of a fault response should be as shown in the example. No variations are allowed, except for the actual `faultCode` and `faultString` values of course.

There is no such thing as an official fault code list; you have to define and document the used fault codes yourself, or use the ones proposed on the Specification for Fault Code Interoperability page[3].

Besides the detailed layout of the XML files and the datatypes defined therein, the spec also mentions that:

- the request must be sent using the HTTP POST method

---

[2] http://ontosys.com/xml-rpc/extensions.php
[3] http://xmlrpc-epi.sourceforge.net/specs/rfc.fault_codes.php

- the request must be sent with correct headers: `Content-type` (which must be "text/xml"), `Content-length`, `Host` and `User-Agent`

Note that you can use basic authentication and HTTPS to protect the XML-RPC service.

Next to the spec, there are four commonly used method calls supported by an XML-RPC server. They all start with "system." which is a namespace considered to be reserved by the server, by convention. This supplement to the original XML-RPC specification is the XML-RPC Introspection spec, implemented by many XML-RPC servers. We will now look at each of these four methods in turn.

system.listMethods

This method, if called, will output a list of methods implemented by the XML-RPC server, and requires no parameters. It will output an array of strings containing the method names, similar to the following:

```
<methodResponse>
    <params>
        <param>
            <value>
                <array>
                    <data>
                        <value><string>system.listMethods</string></value>
                        <!-- other system methods omitted for brevity -->
                        <value><string>zfws.createOrder</string></value>
                        <value><string>zfws.getStockFigures</string></value>
                    </data>
                </array>
            </value>
        </param>
    </params>
</methodResponse>
```

The other system methods should be listed too, as the listing shows only a partial example.

system.methodSignature

More information on an implemented method can be retrieved by calling `system.methodSignature` with the method name as parameter. The result will be an array of possible signatures. These signatures describe the parameters and types that can be used for issuing a call to the method, and should give a developer a hint regarding what is and is not allowed. The signature is an array of types where the first entry is the return type.

An example of `system.methodSignature` is as follows:

```
<methodCall>
    <methodName>system.methodSignature</methodName>
    <params>
        <param>
            <value><string>zfws.getStockFigures/string></value>
        </param>
    </params>
</methodCall>
```

That call will result in a rather deeply-nested response:

```
<methodResponse>
    <params>
        <param>
            <value>
                <array>
                    <data>
                        <value>
                            <array>
                                <data>
                                    <value><string>int</string></value>
                                    <value><string>int</string></value>
                                </data>
                            </array>
                        </value>
                    </data>
                </array>
            </value>
        </param>
    </params>
</methodResponse>
```

Here, only one signature is shown (return value of type "int" followed by the input parameter of type "int"), but multiple signatures are possible in some cases. Suppose that getStockFigures for example accepts strings too, and in that case would return a string, that signature should be added to the outermost <array>.

If a method has no signature defined, a non-array value is returned.

system.methodHelp

This method also takes one parameter, just like system.methodSignature and returns some descriptive documentation on using the method. Note that the resulting output may contain HTML.

system.multicall

This method is actually not part of XML-RPC Introspection, but is used in a few implementations in the wild. It allows for calling multiple methods using only one request, sometimes called *boxcarring*. Multicall accepts an array of XML-RPC calls encoded as structs as follows:

```
<struct>
    <member>
        <name>methodName</name>
        <value><string>zfws.createOrder</string></value>
    </member>
    <member>
        <name>params</name>
        <value><string></string></value>
    </member>
</struct>
```

Multiple structs like the given example are placed in an array and can be sent to system.multicall, which will accept and attempt to execute each one of them.

The result is an array of responses, with a response for each call in the request array. Such a response in this array can be a fault response too. The length of the returned array must always match the length of the request.

The overall response will only be a fault response if something went wrong in the multicall method itself, for example if it is not implemented.

122 ■ XML-RPC

As we will see further in this chapter, Zend Framework's XML-RPC component supports boxcarring through `system.multicall`.

A final note before moving on to some example code: around 2001 an attempt was made to define a standardized set of fault codes[4] but it is not defined as a standard. Some clients and servers use these codes however. Additionally, there was a proposal[5] for a `system.getcapablities` method that could give clients the ability to detect what parts of the spec and add-ons like Introspection, multicall and the proposed fault codes are supported by the XML-RPC server.

XML-RPC and PHP

PHP has mixed support for XML-RPC. There is the XML-RPC extension[6], which exposes a number of XML-RPC-related functions. This extension is not enabled by default, but if you followed the setup guidelines in Chapter 1, your installation should have it enabled. Check the `phpinfo()` output to make sure.

Be aware that this extension is a copy of the XMLRPC-EPI extension[7] for the C language, and that it has been marked experimental for quite some time. The parent EPI library has seen some updates since 2002, the while the PHP extension has not been updated since 2002.

Even more importantly, the extension has only very limited support for the client part of XML-RPC. There are no functions for querying a remote XML-RPC service and automatically converting the response to native PHP typed variables. The icing on the cake is that the documentation on the extension is sparse and incomplete.

Note that an attempt to build a successor[8] for the XML-RPC extension was committed to PECL a few years ago but since, appears to have been abandoned, with no releases since 2005.

There are probably two reasons why XML-RPC support has not become feature-complete, unlike SOAP support. Firstly, successors to XML-RPC, such as SOAP, and other approaches, such as REST, saw a rapid rise in popularity that resulted in a di-

---

[4] http://xmlrpc-epi.sourceforge.net/specs/rfc.fault_codes.php
[5] http://tech.groups.yahoo.com/group/xml-rpc/message/2897
[6] http://php.net/manual/en/book.xmlrpc.php
[7] http://xmlrpc-epi.sourceforge.net
[8] http://pecl.php.net/package/XMLRPCi

minished interest in XML-RPC. Secondly, it is relatively easy to build a PHP-only solution for creating a XML-RPC server and client. Solutions include:

- PHPXMLRPC[9]

- The Incutio XML-RPC library (IXR)[10]

- Keith Devens' XML-RPC library[11]

You could easily come up with your own too, if you would like to do so.

We will try some examples using the XML-RPC PHP extension, but if you are tempted to build a non-Zend Framework-based solution, think twice and consider one of the listed PHP-based libraries. Be aware that the Zend_XmlRpc component can be used without the MVC features of the framework, and its support for different aspects of XML-RPC is probably the best of all solutions available out there.

For the client role in the examples, we will use the supplied sample client code available in the samples/ subdirectory of the XML-RPC extension source code. This solution has been used in other projects too, as a workaround for the limited support for the client part of XML-RPC in the extension. The code is included in the accompanying source code.

Let's have a look at an example XML-RPC server (xmlrpcserver.php), created using the PHP extension:

```
function someMathConstant($methodname, $params, $additional)
{
   $constant = NULL;
   if ($params[0]) {
      $constant = $params[0];
   }
   switch($constant) {
     case 'pi':
        return '3.14159265';
        break;
        return 'unknown variable';
        break;
```

---

[9]http://phpxmlrpc.sourceforge.net/
[10]http://scripts.incutio.com/xmlrpc/
[11]http://keithdevens.com/software/xmlrpc

```
        }
    }

    $xmlrpcserver = xmlrpc_server_create();
    xmlrpc_server_register_method($xmlrpcserver, 'constant', 'someMathConstant');

    $request  = file_get_contents('php://input');
    $response = xmlrpc_server_call_method($xmlrpcserver, $request, '');
    print trim($response); // added trim, to avoid a newline

    xmlrpc_server_destroy($xmlrpcserver);
```

First we created a someMathConstant() function, which accepts three parameters as they will be passed by the XML-RPC server. The server is created using xmlrpc_server_create() and we register our function with the server, the function will be known to the outside world as "constant". The incoming request is read and handed over to the server using xmlrpc_server_call_method(). The result is printed so the XML-RPC client can read the output, the server resource is destroyed afterwards.

A bit clumsy, indeed: We had to adapt the someMathConstant() function we used in previous examples to accept more parameters, not all of which are even necessary for the function to create some useful output.

Note that object methods can be registered too:

```
    class someMath
    {
        public function someMathConstant($methodname, $params, $additional)
        {
            $constant = NULL;
            if ($params[0]) {
                $constant = $params[0];
            }
            switch($constant) {
                // ...
            }
        }
    }

    $xmlrpcserver = xmlrpc_server_create();
    $math = new someMath();
```

```
xmlrpc_server_register_method($xmlrpcserver, 'constant', array(&$math, '
    someMathConstant'));

$request = file_get_contents('php://input');
$response = xmlrpc_server_call_method($xmlrpcserver, $request, '');
print trim($response);

xmlrpc_server_destroy($xmlrpcserver);
```

Let us first fire a request at this server using the XML-RPC utilities library found in the XML-RPC samples directory:

```
include("xmlrpcutils/utils.php");
$result = xu_rpc_http_concise(
   array(
      'method' => 'constant',
      'args'   => 'pi',
      'host'   => 'zfws',
      'uri'    => '/xmlrpcserver.php',
      'port'   => 80
   )
);

if (xmlrpc_is_fault($result)) {
   echo 'Fault: [' . $result['faultCode'] . '] ' . $result['faultString'];
} else {
   echo '<pre>' . $result . '</pre>';
}
```

The xu_rpc_http_concise() function accepts an options array, creates the necessary XML and posts it to the specified URI endpoint. It returns a PHP array, decoded from the resulting XML received from the server.

The output of the above code would read "3.14159265". Change the "method" parameter to "constant2" and you will see:

```
Fault: [-32601] server error. method not found. constant2
```

We will not go into further detail on the xu_* set of functions. They are somewhat convenient, but limited. As an alternative, we could have done this by using

Zend_Http_Client, and accessing the XML response. The resulting XML would look like the following structure:

```
<?xml version="1.0" encoding="iso-8859-1"?>
<methodResponse>
    <params>
        <param>
            <value><string>3.14159265</string></value>
        </param>
    </params>
</methodResponse>
```

There is no out-of-the-box support for system.ListMethods and the other mentioned system calls.

Note that several debuggers for testing XML-RPC calls to your server are available online. A debugger can be a handy tool in case you need to debug something from a remote location.

Creating the XML-RPC Service Using Zend Framework

From previous paragraphs it should be clear that Zend Framework's Zend_XmlRpc component does not use the XML-RPC extension. It does support the four system methods mentioned before, but not the system.getcapablities method. You can have a peek at Zend_XmlRpc_Server_System to see how this support is implemented.

Zend_XmlRpc_Server

Like most, if not all, Zend Framework server classes, using Zend_XmlRpc_Server is similar to using PHP's SoapServer class. Launching it is as simple as:

```
$server = new Zend_XmlRpc_Server();
$server->setClass('MTA_Service', 'zfws');
echo $server->handle();
```

The setClass() method also accepts an object as its first argument, which results in that object being assigned to handle the XML-RPC request. The server can accept functions too, using addFunction(). The second argument to setClass() is optional, and specifies a namespace:

```
$server->addFunction('someMathConstant', 'math');
```

By default, Zend_XmlRpc_Server will use the request read from php://input. You can set the request data yourself by passing a Zend_XmlRpc_Request object, or an instance of a subclass of Zend_XmlRpc_Request, to Zend_XmlRpc_Server::handle().

If the request is successful, the result returned is a Zend_XmlRpc_Response object by default, though this can be altered using Zend+XmlRpc_Server::setResponseClass(). In case of failure, a Zend_XmlRpc_Server_Fault object instance is returned. These classes all have __toString() methods, so simply printing the returned result makes the XML output available to the client.

Remember that we can add the code for bootstrapping our XML-RPC server to the more general API.php file too, adding an Xmlrpc_Bootstrap class to the ServiceBootstrap.php file, just as we did for SOAP.

Zend_XmlRpc_Client

Let us try out a client call to system.listmethods:

```
require_once('Zend/Loader.php');
Zend_Loader::loadClass('Zend_XmlRpc_Client');
$client = new Zend_XmlRpc_Client('http://zfws/XMLRPC.php');
$result = $client->call('system.listMethods');
print_r($result);
```

The resulting array will contain method names including the system.* methods and zfws.getCatalogue, zfws.getStockFigures and so on.

There is an alternative approach, using the getProxy() which "virtualizes" the access to the server. In other words, this method returns an object that allows us to use the available XML-RPC methods as if they are local to that object. The object in fact represents the server and its exposed methods and using it provides a more convenient means of talking to the server. For example:

```
$result = $client->getProxy()->system->listMethods();
```

Passing an argument is done like this:

```
$result = $client->call('zfws.getStockFigures', array(1));

// or

$result = $client->getProxy()->zfws->getStockFigures(1);
```

A call to:

```
$result = $client->getProxy()->system->methodHelp('zfws.getStockFigures');
```

Results in:

```
Returns number of items in stock for the product.
```

The above line was added as the first line of the docblock for Mta_Service::getStockFigures().

If you need access to the response and request objects from the client side, then the getLastRequest() and getLastResponse() methods could prove invaluable:

```
$request = new Zend_XmlRpc_Request();
$request->setMethod('zfws.getStockFigures');
$request->setParams(array(1));
$result = $client->doRequest($request);
echo '<pre>';
print_r($client->getLastRequest());
print_r($client->getLastResponse());
echo '</pre>';
```

Doing so, you are able to inspect what is sent and received. A call to the third system method system.methodSignature:

```
$result = $client->getProxy()->system->methodSignature('zfws.getStockFigures');
```

Results in the following output:

```
Array
(
    [0] => Array
        (
            [returnType] => int
            [parameters] => Array
                (
                    [0] => int
                )
        )
)
```

The outer array contains only one member, since we defined only one signature for this method. No variations are possible for this method. Note that Zend_XmlRpc clearly sets apart the return type and the parameters.

Zend_XmlRpc gets this information from the docblocks accompanying your methods, so make sure they are in a healthy state. You can add XML-RPC specific types next to already existing ones. Suppose you have a method with a string parameter, and you know that this string is a date in a specific format, you can augment the content of the @param tag like so:

```
/**
 * some explanation here
 *
 * @param string|dateTime.iso8601  $timestamp
 * @return bool
 */
```

This is safe because phpDocumentor will ignore types that it does not recognize. There are some nice additional tricks available, such as Zend_XmlRpc recognizing a @param defined as a Zend_Date as being an XML-RPC dateTime.iso8601 type.

Fault responses are handled by Zend_XmlRpc_Client on the client side on several possible levels. A Zend_XmlRpc_Client_HttpException exception is thrown when an HTTP error is met (like a 404) and a Zend_XmlRpc_Client_FaultException is thrown when an XML-RPC fault messages is received. A network error or DNS error results in a Zend_Http_Client_Adapter_Exception. You can catch all of them as follows:

```
try {
```

130 ■ XML-RPC

```
    $client = new Zend_XmlRpc_Client('http://zfws/XMLRPC.php');
    $result = $client->call('system.listMethods');
} catch (Exception $e) {
  echo $e->getCode();
  echo $e->getMessage();
  echo get_class($e);
}
```

Or differentiate between them:

```
try {
   $client = new Zend_XmlRpc_Client('http://zfws/XMLRPC.php');
   $result = $client->call('system.listMethods');
} catch (Zend_XmlRpc_Client_FaultException $e) {
   echo get_class($e) . ': [' . $e->getCode() . '] ' . $e->getMessage();
} catch (Zend_XmlRpc_Client_HttpException $e) {
   echo get_class($e) . ': [' . $e->getCode() . '] ' . $e->getMessage();
} catch (Zend_Http_Client_Adapter_Exception $e) {
   echo get_class($e) . ': [' . $e->getCode() . '] ' . $e->getMessage();
}
```

Playing with the method name, hostname and the PHP script filename being called results in different errors being displayed on your screen.

Finally, let us try a multicall example:

```
$result = $client->call('system.multicall',
                array(
                    array(
                        array(
                            'methodName' => 'zfws.getStockFigures',
                            'params'     => array(1)
                        ),
                        array(
                            'methodName' => 'zfws.getOrderStatus',
                            'params'     => array(1)
                        )
                    )
                )
            );
```

That call will result in:

```
Array
(
    [0] => 111
    [1] => shipped
)
```

Multicall is an interesting approach, as it allows for sending multiple requests with one call, and by doing so saves you some roundtrip time.

More Zend_XmlRpc_Server

Some more advanced things you should know about the server part should be mentioned.

Multiple Namespaces

You can assign more than one class using the provided namespaces:

```
$server->setClass('Mta_Service', 'zfws');      // zfws.* methods
$server->setClass('Something_Else', 'other');  // other.* methods
echo $server->handle();
```

Encoding

The server's default UTF-8 encoding can be retrieved and changed through `Zend_XmlRpc_Server::getEncoding()` and `Zend_XmlRpc_Server::setEncoding()`. In case some client requires it, you could set "iso-8859-1" as the encoding for example.

Faultcodes and Exceptions

`Zend_XmlRpc_Server` catches exceptions generated by a method it calls as the result of an incoming request. An XML-RPC fault response is generated based on this exception, but not all information is passed since some information could be sensitive. You can whitelist your own exception classes to be passed through using:

```
Zend_XmlRpc_Server_Fault::attachFaultException('Mta_Exception');
```

We can throw this `Mta_Exception` exception in case we detect an error:

```
public function getStockFigures($product_id)
{
   if ($product_id > 0) {
     Zend_Loader::loadFile(APPLICATION_PATH . '/models/Stock.php');
     $stock = new Mta_Model_Stock();
     return $stock->getAvailable($product_id);
   } else {
      throw new Mta_Exception('Product id must be lt 0','888');
   }
}
```

This call:

```
try {
   $result = $client->getProxy()->zfws->getStockFigures(0);
   echo '<pre>';
   print_r($result);
   echo '</pre>';
} catch (Exception $e) {
   echo get_class($e).' ['.$e->getCode().'] '.$e->getMessage();
}
```

Will result in "Zend_XmlRpc_Client_FaultException [888] Product id must be greater than 0". You can extend this to send faults when, for example, someone tries to retrieve a non-existent piece of information or does something that is not allowed with the specified data. The error codes used in the exception will show up as the faultCode in the response: A neat way to pass and reuse your already existing exceptions.

Caching

Two possible performance improvements can be applied when firing up your server. Firstly, the `Zend_XmlRpc_Server_Cache` class allows caching of server definitions:

```
$cacheFile = dirname(__FILE__) . '/../data/cache/xmlrpc.cache';
$server = new Zend_XmlRpc_Server();
```

```
if (!Zend_XmlRpc_Server_Cache::get($cacheFile, $server)) {
    Zend_Loader::loadClass('Mta_Service');
    $server->setClass('MTA_Service','zfws');
    Zend_XmlRpc_Server_Cache::save($cacheFile, $server);
}
echo $server->handle();
```

This way, the class information will not have to be loaded on each request, since some of the reflection information can be cached like this.

XML Generation

Another optimization possible is to override the default XML generation strategy. which uses `DomDocument`. PHP's `XMLWriter` can be used instead by setting `Zend_XmlRpc_Generator_XMLWriter` as the generator:

```
Zend_XmlRpc_Value::setGenerator(new Zend_XmlRpc_Generator_XMLWriter());
$server = new Zend_XmlRpc_Server();
```

Customizing the XML-RPC Service

In previous chapters we explained in detail how to meet the requirements, especially the necessary customizations for every Zend Framework component being discussed. This chapter and the next chapter will be much shorter in that respect, since the solutions discussed here would result in duplicating already explained code and ideas if they would be elaborated into detail.

API version in the URL

We placed our code in `XMLRPC.php`, just like the preferred SOAP solution outside the MVC flow and outside a controller. This means that you could use URL rewriting and have `/XMLRPC/v1.0` or `/v1.0/XMLRPC` point to `XMLRPC.php?v=1.0` for example.

Depending on the `$_GET['v']` parameter, another class can be assigned to the XML-RPC server.

As an alternative, you could use the version number in your namespace:

134 ■ XML-RPC

```
$server->setClass('Mta_Service', 'zfws');        // zfws.* methods
$server->setClass('Mta_Service_Advanced', 'zfws20'); // zfws20.* methods
echo $server->handle();
```

API Key and Pre-processing

Since we can set the request object using `handle($request)` we are able to parse the request and check for a valid API key before actually handing it over to the server.

The client request can be adapted like the XML request listed here. Note that the API key "123456" is added as the first parameter.

```
<?xml version="1.0" encoding="UTF-8"?>
<methodCall>
  <methodName>zfws.getStockFigures</methodName>
  <params>
    <param><value>123456</value></param>
    <param><value><int>1</int></value></param>
  </params>
</methodCall>
```

POSTing this XML (as `$xml`) to the adapted XML-RPC server can be done using `Zend_Http_Client` or `Zend_XmlRpc_Client`:

```
$client = new Zend_Http_Client('http://zfws/XMLRPCbis.php');
$response = $client->setRawData($xml, 'text/xml')->request('POST');
```

In `XMLRPCbis.php` we are able check and strip the API key from the incoming request:

```
$data = file_get_contents('php://input');
$dom = new DOMDocument();
$server = new Zend_XmlRpc_Server();

if (!$dom->loadXML((string) $data)) {
   echo $server->fault('Invalid XML',400);
} else {
   $xml = simplexml_load_string((string) $data);
   if (isset($xml->params) && isset($xml->params->param[0])) {
      // check access for key
      //... here we should check access for the API key in
```

```
        //... $xml->params->param[0]
        //... if no access return 403

        // then strip it out
        unset($xml->params->param[0]);
        $xmlstring = (string) $xml->asXml();

        // remove whitespace & empty lines
        $str = trim($string);
        $str = preg_replace("/(^[\r\n]*|[\r\n]+)[\s\t]*[\r\n]+/", "\n", $str);

        $request = new Zend_XmlRpc_Request();
        $request->loadXml($str);
        echo $server->handle($request);
    } else {
        echo $server->fault('Missing API key',403);
    }
}
```

What happens here is this:

- the incoming XML is checked to see if it is well-formed. If not a fault response is sent

- the XML string is imported as a `SimpleXMLElement` object -the first parameter is considered to be the API key, access is checked

- the API key is stripped out, resulting whitespace in the XML string is removed

- finally the request XML is handed over to the server

The above code was added just to show a solution. This could be elaborated further, like the example code given in the SOAP chapters. Variations and other solutions are possible too of course.

Summary

- We know what XML-RPC means and how to create and consume a XML-RPC service using PHP and Zend Framework

- We have a clue as to how to customize the XML-RPC server

Deliverables:

- We created a basic XML-RPC server that can be refined, and already checks and accepts API keys for each request

Chapter 7

JSON-RPC

Introduction

JSON-RPC is another RPC-oriented protocol, and although the overall concept resembles XML-RPC, there are many differences:

- data is encoded using JSON (JavaScript Object Notation), a human-readable format which is able to represent objects and arrays

- transport is mostly performed over HTTP, but the use of TCP/IP sockets is also encouraged

- client and server can treat each other as peers, calling each other's methods and sending notifications to one another

There are two main versions of JSON-RPC: 1.0[1] and the proposed 2.0[2] which is not yet considered official. Zend Framework's Zend_Json_Server has support for both.

Because of the JSON encoding, JSON-RPC has a lot of potential in the Web 2.0 sphere where responsive web-based interfaces that use a combination of client and server side techniques dominate. The ability to use straight TCP/IP sockets, with less overhead, is an additional advantage.

---

[1] http://json-rpc.org/wiki/specification
[2] http://groups.google.com/group/json-rpc/web/json-rpc-2-0

For version 1.0, a JSON-RPC request to a service has three properties:

- **method:** a string with the remote method name
- **params:** an array of objects being passed as arguments to the method
- **id:** a request id, used for matching request and response

A response also has three properties:

- **result:** the object returned by the method. Null in case of error
- **error:** an error object. Must be null in case of no error
- **id:** must match the id send by the client peer

A response can only be sent as the result of a request.

There is also a special type of request, called a **notification**. Notifications are similar to requests, but no response is expected and the "id" property must be null.

We will now turn to some specifics on the type of transport.

Streams

JSON-RPC communication can be sent over TCP/IP socket streams. Closing the connection between the peers must raise an exception if there are outstanding requests without response.

HTTP

Since HTTP typically is a client-server communication protocol, there are some limitations. To allow the server-side peer to send messages to the client, the client may send empty HTTP POST requests to eventually pick up a request sent by the server. Invalid requests must close the connection and invalid responses must raise an exception if there are unanswered questions on the client side. This sounds straightforward, but is unfortunately not particularly easy to implement.

JSON-RPC 2.0 requests and response are not guaranteed to work with version 1.0 clients and servers. The 2.0 version differs from 1.0 in these areas:

Request

An additional parameter, "jsonrpc", is added. This specifies the version and contains the value "2.0". Some rules are added for the existing parameters:

- **method:** method names cannot start with "rpc.", as these are reserved for optional system extensions
- **params:** may be omitted, so becomes optional
- **id:** a string or number without decimal fractions. May be Null but this is discouraged

Response

As with the request, an additional parameter is added, "jsonrpc", which specifies the version and contains the value "2.0". Some additional rules exist for the parameters:

- **result:** must not exist in case of an error
- **error:** must not exist in case of no error
- **id:** if an error occurred in detecting the id in the request, this must be Null

Error Object

An error object to be used is defined as having these parameters:

- **code:** must be an integer
- **message:** short description, a single sentence
- **data:** more information on the error can appear here. This can be a string, an array, an object, or may be omitted entirely

The -32768 to -32000 range of error codes is reserved for pre-defined errors. Currently the following error codes are defined:

```
-32700          Parse error         invalid JSON received
-32600          Invalid Request     not a valid Request object
-32601          Method not found    method does not exist / is not available
-32602          Invalid params      invalid method parameter(s)
-32603          Internal error      internal JSON-RPC error
-32099 to -32000 Server error       reserved for implementation-defined errors
```

Any other codes in this range are available for application specific errors.

Batches

The client is allowed to send a batch of requests as an array with request objects. The server should respond with an array of responses. Notifications, if received in the request batch, will not have a corresponding response object in the response batch. If only notifications were sent in the request, the server should return no response.

The server is allowed to process the batch in parallel, so you cannot expect the requests being handled in a certain order. You cannot even expect the response array to be in the same order as the request array. Matching of objects should be done based on the IDs. As you may have noticed, all this faintly resembles the XML-RPC `system.multicall` method.

The batch response can be a single response object, in case the batch call itself fails.

An interesting evolution is the JSON-RPC related Service Mapping Description Proposal[3]. This proposal details how to describe a JSON-RPC service but could also be used to describe a REST service. The proposal describes the transport mechanism, message envelope and available methods for a given web service; and uses JSON to represent the information. We will show an example later on in this chapter.

JSON-RPC and PHP

There is no such thing as a JSON-RPC extension or standard solution for JSON-RPC support in PHP. Implementing a library yourself should be possible of course, but it would require quite an effort if you want to do it right.

---
[3] http://groups.google.com/group/json-schema/web/service-mapping-description-proposal

There are some PHP-based solutions that can help-such as PHP-O-Lait[4] and json-rpc2php[5]. In addition, the previously mentioned PHPXMLRPC library also has beta support for JSON-RPC.

While there is no standard solution, Zend Framework fortunately offers some JSON-RPC related classes, as part of the Zend_Json component. The two most notable ones are Zend_Json_Server and Zend_Json_Server_Smd.

Zend_Json_Server

Zend_Json_Server, Zend Framework's JSON server class is part of Zend_Json and supports both JSON-RPC versions 1.0 and 2.0. The component provides a similar API to Zend_XmlRpc_Server, so this sample code should seem quite familiar from the previous chapters:

```
$server = new Zend_Json_Server();
$server->setClass('Mta_Service');
$server->handle();
```

Zend_Json_Server listens to POST requests only. The request object used is instantiated internally from Zend_Json_Server_Request and the response consists of a Zend_Json_Server_Response object which implements __toString(), and so can be printed directly.

Setting and manipulating the request and response can be done just like in the previous chapters. Handing a Zend_Json_Server_Request object to handle() allows for fine tuning the incoming request first and setting Zend_Json_Server::setAutoEmitResponse(false) will cause handle() to return a Zend_Json_Server_Response object instead of emitting it directly. In this way, the request and response can both be inspected and modified.

There are HTTP-specific versions of the request and response objects, Zend_Json_Server_Request_Http and Zend_Json_Server_Response_Http. The first will read its input from the php://input stream and the latter will send output with correct HTTP response headers.

---

[4]http://phpolait.sourceforge.net
[5]http://code.google.com/p/jsonrpc2php

```
$server = new Zend_Json_Server();
$server->setClass('Mta_Service');
$request = new Zend_Json_Server_Request_Http();
$server->setAutoEmitResponse(false);
//returns a Zend_Json_Server_Response_Http object
$response = $server->handle($request);
echo $response;
```

Issuing a JSON-RPC compliant call using a `Zend_Http_Client` client can be fairly straightforward:

```
$request = new stdClass();
$request->jsonrpc = '2.0';
$request->method = 'getStockFigures';
$request->params = array('id' => 1);
$request->id = time();

$json = Zend_Json::encode($request);

$client = new Zend_Http_Client('http://zfws/JSONRPC.php');
$response = $client->setRawData($json, 'application/json')->request('POST');
```

The resulting request that is sent is this:

```
{
    "jsonrpc":"2.0",
    "method":"getStockFigures",
    "params":[ 1 ],
    "id":1271704823
}
```

And the response we receive is as follows:

```
{
    "result":111,
    "id":"1271704823",
    "error":null,
    "jsonrpc":"2.0"
}
```

If `Zend_Json_Server` encounters an error, a `Zend_Json_Server_Error` object is sent in the response. Suppose you call a nonexistent method, the response would look like the following:

```
{
   "result":null,
   "error":{
      "code":-32601,
      "message":"Method not found",
      "data":null
   },
   "id":"1271706538",
   "jsonrpc":"2.0"
}
```

`Zend_Json_Server_Error` has three properties: an error code, a short error message, and finally some additional data; all this following the JSON-RPC specification.

Remember that we can add the code for bootstrapping a JSON-RPC server to the more general `API.php` file too, adding an `Jsonrpc_Bootstrap` class to the `ServiceBootstrap.php` file, just as we did for SOAP before.

Zend_Json_Server_Smd

`Zend_Json_Server_Smd` allows you to add support for the proposed Service Mapping Description standard:

```
$server = new Zend_Json_Server();
$server->setClass('Mta_Service');
if ('GET' == $_SERVER['REQUEST_METHOD']) {
   $server->setTarget('/JSONRPC.php')
          ->setEnvelope(Zend_Json_Server_Smd::ENV_JSONRPC_2);
   $smd = $server->getServiceMap();
   header('Content-Type: application/json');
   echo $smd;
   return;
}
$server->handle();
```

By commenting out the `header()` function call which sends the "application/json" content-type header, and browsing to the `http://zfws/JSONRPC.php` server you will see the generated SMD description object, with some description for the methods exposed through the `Mta_Service` class. As we will see further on, SMD allows for integration with JSON-RPC-aware JavaScript libraries such as Dojo.

As always with HTTP requests, you could have retrieved the SMD information using `Zend_Http_Client` too:

```
$client = new Zend_Http_Client('http://zfws/JSONRPC.php');
$response = $client->request('GET');
```

The resulting $response will contain a string with a JSON representation of the SMD.

Analogous to `Zend_XmlRpc_Server_Cache`, there is a `Zend_Json_Server_Cache`, which will cache the SMD information created by the server using Zend Framework's `Zend_Server_Reflection`. Some performance gain can be achieved using `Zend_Json_Server_Cache`. It works a little differently from `Zend_XmlRpc_Server_Cache` which returns the complete server if a match is found in the cache. `Zend_Json_Server_Cache` is designed for caching the SMD information, rather than the entire server.

```
$cacheFile = dirname(__FILE__) . '/../data/cache/jsonrpc.cache';
$server = new Zend_Json_Server();

Zend_Loader::loadClass('Mta_Service');
$server->setClass('MTA_Service');

if ('GET' == $_SERVER['REQUEST_METHOD']) {
    if (!($smd = Zend_Json_Server_Cache::getSmd($cacheFile, $server))) {
        Zend_Json_Server_Cache::saveSmd($cacheFile, $server);
        $smd = $server->getServiceMap();
    }
    $server->setTarget('/JSONRPCbis.php');
    header('Content-Type: application/json');
    echo $smd;
    return;
}
$server->handle();
```

This will result in the internal service map being cached as an SMD file in the specified cache file, and retrieved from the cache without all those expensive reflection calls that are used to build it in the first instance.

Connecting from JavaScript

What makes JSON-RPC particularly interesting is the powerful combination of JavaScript libraries that support JSON-RPC and a server side component. To give you an idea of what could be possible; two short and simple examples using Dojo and jQuery are included here.

We'll start with Dojo, and add a Zend Framework controller named `AjaxController`, with the action method `dojotestAction()`, and corresponding view scripts. The view script `application/views/scripts/ajax/dojotest.phtml` looks like the following:

```
<!DOCTYPE html PUBLIC "-//W3C//DTD XHTML 1.0 Strict//EN"
    "http://www.w3.org/TR/xhtml1/DTD/xhtml1-strict.dtd">
<html xmlns="http://www.w3.org/1999/xhtml" xml:lang="en" lang="en">
<head>
    <script src="... dojo.js at google cdn ..."></script>
    <script type="text/javascript">
       dojo.require('dojo.rpc.JsonService');
       var proxy;
       function setup() {
          proxy = new dojo.rpc.JsonService('http://zfws/JSONRPCdojo.php');
       }

       function getData() {
          inputvalue = document.getElementById('productid').value;
          var result = proxy.getStockFigures(inputvalue).addCallback(print);
       }

       function print(result) {
          //alert(result);
          node = dojo.byId("result");
          node.innerHTML = result;
       }

       dojo.addOnLoad(setup);
    </script>

</head>
<body>
<div id="welcome">
    <h1>A Dojo test with JSON-RPC</h1>
    Available stock: <div id="result"></div>
    For product with id: <input type="text" id="productid" value="1" />
```

```
        <button onclick="getData();">Get the data</button> You can try 1, 2 and 3 for
            different results.
</div>
</body>
</html>
```

Please note that we had to add this line in the code instantiating the server side:

```
$smd->setDojoCompatible(true);
```

This allows the SMD object to output Dojo-compatible information. Remember that SMD is not yet a standard, so that this allows for supporting the Dojo-specific interpretation of the expected standard.

What will happen is this:

- the Dojo library is loaded from Google's Content Delivery Network (CDN)
- the required JSON-RPC classes are loaded and a proxy object pointing to the SMD output is created on document load
- clicking the button will fire `getData()` with the product ID taken from the input field
- the proxy object talks to the exposed `getStockFigures()` method, and receives the stock information

You can test it by pointing your browser at `http://zfws/ajax/dojotest`. Remember that you must have internet access for the Dojo library to be loaded from Google's CDN.

This is only a trivial example, but with a bit of imagination some powerful user interfaces can be built using Dojo and `Zend_Json_Server`.

For those preferring jQuery, you can use the Zend Framework RPC plugin[6]. This plugin, together with the `json2.js` library used for interpreting incoming strings as JSON can also be used together with `Zend_Json_Server` output.

---
[6] http://plugins.jquery.com/project/zendjsonrpc

```html
<!DOCTYPE html PUBLIC "-//W3C//DTD XHTML 1.0 Strict//EN"
    "http://www.w3.org/TR/xhtml1/DTD/xhtml1-strict.dtd">
<html xmlns="http://www.w3.org/1999/xhtml" xml:lang="en" lang="en">
<head>
    <script type="text/javascript" src="/js/jquery-1.3.min.js"></script>
    <script type="text/javascript" src="/js/json2.js"></script>
    <script type="text/javascript" src="/js/jquery.zend.jsonrpc.js"></script>
    <script type="text/javascript">

    </script>
</head>
<body>
<div id="welcome">
    <h1>A jQuery test with JSON-RPC</h1>
    Available stock: <div id="result"></div>
    For product with id: <input type="text" id="productid" value="1" />
    <button onclick="getData();">Get the data</button>
    You can try 1, 2 and 3 for different results.
</div>
<script type="text/javascript">
    function getData() {
        proxy = jQuery.Zend.jsonrpc({url: '/JSONRPCbis.php'});
        inputvalue = document.getElementById('productid').value;
        result = proxy.getStockFigures(inputvalue);
        $('#result').text(result);
    }
</script>
</body>
</html>
```

The behavior here is essentially the same as for the Dojo example. The SMD info is retrieved and a call to `getStockFigures()` is issued, and the result is displayed on the page. The above was not elaborated in detail, but it should give you a head start.

What is Missing?

`Zend_Json_Server` does not fully support the JSON-RPC 2.0 spec. For example, there is no complete support for the peer-to-peer aspect of JSON-RPC, at least not at the time of writing. Other features that are missing include the handling of batch calls, and a `Zend_Json_Client` class. Judging from the discussions recently, however this could be added very soon. Example source code[7] is already available and looks very promising. The code is based on the `Zend_XmlRpc_Client` class. A patched `Zend_Json_Server` with batch support can be found there too. Let us hope these proposed pieces of code are merged into the framework soon.

Customize the JSON-RPC Service

Solutions for the two previously discussed customizations are very similar to those suggested in the previous chapter. Just like the XML-RPC solution, you can use URL rewriting and the loading of different classes based on the version in the URL to support multiple versions of the API.

Pre-parsing and checking an incoming request for valid API key can be achieved even more easily:

```
$server = new Zend_Json_Server();

Zend_Loader::loadClass('Mta_Service');
$server->setClass('MTA_Service');

$request = new Zend_Json_Server_Request_Http();
$params = $request->getParams();
if (isset($params[0]) && isset($params[0]['apikey'])) {
   //check access for key
   if ($params[0]['apikey'] == '123456') {
      $request->setParams($params[1]);
   } else {
      $server->fault('Not allowed','',
                     'API key ' . $params[0]['apikey'] . ' not allowed');
   }
}
$server->handle($request);
```

A call like this would be allowed to pass through:

```
$request = new stdClass();
$request->jsonrpc = '2.0';
$request->method = 'getStockFigures';
```

---

[7] http://svn.tine20.org/svn/trunk/tine20/Zend/Json

```
$request->params = array(array('apikey' => 123456), array(1));
$request->id = time();

$client = new Zend_Http_Client('http://zfws/JSONRPCtris.php');
$response = $client->setRawData($json, 'application/json')->request('POST');
```

Changing the API key to 1234567 would result in the following response:

```
{
    "result":null,
    "error":{
        "code":-32000,
        "message":"Not allowed",
        "data":"API key 1234567 not allowed"
    },
    "id":"1271707970",
    "jsonrpc":"2.0"
}
```

Of course, checking of the API key should be replaced with something more meaningful and flexible instead of the hardcoded check for a fixed key shown above.

Summary

- We know what JSON-RPC means and how to create and consume a JSON-RPC service using PHP and Zend Framework
- We have some ideas on how to customize the JSON-RPC server
- Some JavaScript was added into the mix

Deliverables:

- We created a basic JSON-RPC server that can be refined further. A basic API key check was added

Chapter 8

Limiting Access using Zend_Acl

Zend_Acl is a Zend Framework component that allows for defining rules and checking access to resources based on these rules. Rules specify which roles are allowed or denied access to a resource or to a privilege on a resource. This sounds complex, but in fact it is not that hard once you grasp the concept.

Zend Framework has the `Zend_Acl` object which combines all of the above in a single object that can be used throughout your code.

```
$acl = new Zend_Acl();
```

Resources

Resources are parts of your application or business logic such as a controller, a model, a form, an order, a collection of images or a single image. Anything you define a resource for and check access to can be considered a resource. The Zend Framework class for creating and defining a resource is `Zend_Acl_Resource`.

Adding a resource to the ACL object we created above is very simple:

```
$acl->addResource('api');
```

Inside `addResource()` a `Zend_Acl_Resource` object is created using "api" as its ID. We could have passed an instance of `Zend_Acl_Resource`, or an instance of a class which extends it, to `addResource()` too, if we had custom defined resource objects. In our code, we will stick to the default `Zend_Acl_Resource` class and assign our resources as strings.

Resources are actually represented with a tree structure. Child nodes are attached to a single parent node, the root node branching out into individual leaves. Suppose we had another resource, "rest" for example, that could be considered a child to the "api" resource, then adding it as a child resource to the "api" resource can be done like this:

```
$acl->addResource('rest', 'api');
```

Just like "rest", the other web services we created in previous chapters like "soap", "jsonrpc" and "xmlrpc" could be considered children to the "api" resource too. Resources inherit from their ancestors, up to the root node. If a role is allowed access to the root node, and no other rules are defined that affect the role, all child nodes for that root are accessible for the role.

Roles

A role is typically linked to your user profile. In an application, example roles could be:

- an administrator or admin
- external user, for example part of a client company
- internal user, for example part of our own company
- anonymous, a user role for users unknown to the application

An example role, in our case, could be "customer", a role linked to user accounts creating new orders through our web service where calls originate from their own websites:

```
$acl->addRole('customer');
```

We added the role as a string, so inside addRole() a Zend_Acl_Role object is created, and this string is used as the identifier for the object. As previously mentioned, we could alternatively have passed a Zend_Acl_Role instance to addRole().

Roles can inherit from other roles, even from multiple ones. This allows for the combination of roles for different and separate parts of an application into a more global role. In a modular Zend Framework application for example, roles could be matched to modules and application-wide roles could be created using combinations of these roles.

A role used for defining access rules for anonymous users could be added:

```
$acl->addRole('anonymous');
```

We define one more role, "finance department", for internal users from the finance department, querying our service using a reporting interface:

```
$acl->addRole('finance department', 'reports');
```

For the record, as we did not create a reporting tool or module, the above is just for the sake of the example. Now we can add a new role "admin", inheriting from both "customer" and "finance department":

```
$acl->addRole('admin', array('customer', 'finance department'));
```

The "admin" role will inherit rules from both "finance department" and "customer" roles. In our examples, we will not use inheritance between roles in order to keep things less complicated. Keep in mind that if you do choose to inherit from multiple roles, the order in which they are defined is important since rules for the ancestor roles may contradict each other.

Rules

These rules are added for the roles we mentioned:

```
$acl->deny('anonymous', 'api');
$acl->deny('anonymous', 'reports');

$acl->allow('customer', 'api');
$acl->allow('finance department', 'reports');
```

What do they actually mean? We deny access by a user with the "anonymous" role on the API and on the reports. We allow access to the API for the "customer" role, and people working in the finance department will have access to reports, as long as they have that role associated with their account. No explicit rules are defined for our "admin" role for now, it just inherits rules from the "customer" and "finance department" roles.

Privileges

Resources can be approached in multiple ways. For example, a form can have a "view" privilege and a "submit" privilege. An order in our system could have up to four privileges: create, read, update and delete (or POST, GET, PUT and DELETE for REST). These privileges allow for even more refined rules to be defined. You can add them as the third parameter in the allow() method:

```
$acl->allow('customer', 'order', 'create');
```

Now our "customer" role has the "create" privilege on the "order" resource. You can also just omit privileges from the rules, as the examples above did not use them. We are going to use them in our example code later in this chapter, however.

Checking access using Zend_Acl is simple too:

```
echo $acl->isAllowed('anonymous', 'rest') ? 'allowed' : 'denied';
echo $acl->isAllowed('customer', 'rest') ? 'allowed' : 'denied';
echo $acl->isAllowed('customer', 'soap') ? 'allowed' : 'denied';
echo $acl->isAllowed('finance department', 'reports') ? 'allowed' : 'denied';
echo $acl->isAllowed('finance department', 'jsonrpc') ? 'allowed' : 'denied';
echo $acl->isAllowed('admin', 'xmlrpc') ? 'allowed' : 'denied';
```

This will result in:

```
anonymous            -> rest:    denied
customer             -> rest:    allowed
customer             -> soap:    allowed
finance department   -> reports: allowed
finance department   -> jsonrpc: denied
admin                -> xmlrpc:  allowed
```

All of the above and other examples are available for testing in the `public/acltest.php` file. In case you would like to deny access to a certain resource for everyone, you can just use NULL instead of the roles:

```
$acl->deny(NULL, 'admin');
```

This will block anyone trying to access the administration interface, if there were one, and if the check for the rules were to be added there, of course. You can do the same for the resource too, denying for example everyone known in the past as abusers of the system:

```
$acl->deny('abusers', NULL);
```

You can also just omit the NULL in the above line of code.

Zend_Acl does not enforce a standard method of implementing an ACL in your application; it just supplies you with a set of tools to handle all of this using just a few lines of code.

Further benefits include the fact that you can instantiate a Zend_Acl with a Zend_Config object. This means you can define roles, rules, privileges and resources using a .ini or XML file for permanent storage. In addition, Zend_Acl is designed to survive serialization and being saved as a string. Recreating it from a serialized string format will restore all of its functionality.

That last point is important because it means you can store the entire object in your session, or in a cache backend that supports serialization, and fetch and use it whenever necessary. Storing PHP values in Memcached for example will often result in objects like Zend_Acl instances automatically being serialized using PHP's serialize() before being written to the cache. If a resource such as a database connection would have been used inside a Zend_Acl object, then serialization and restoring would not have been that simple.

Note that you can also create conditional checks and have them applied to rules. We are not going to explore it further, but this approach makes it possible to deny access for example during the night, when backups are being done (assuming your business allows for being offline for a short time, of course).

Where to Store the Rules

Adding and defining rules, roles and resources in your existing code can take up a lot of extra lines in your code and do not necessarily make that code easier to understand. It is possible to store these building blocks for the `Zend_Acl` object somewhere for persistence and restore and load them on the fly when necessary. For performance reasons, a cached version could be used instead if it exists.

If we would save these items in the database for example, we could extend `Zend_Acl` and load resources, roles and rules from the database the first time it is created.

We could also save this information in a .ini file, XML file or even a flat text file, but the database seems an obvious choice, since we already have a bunch of application data stored there. We need five extra tables for this, with the following columns:

acl_roles:

- `role_id`
- `role_name`

acl_resources:

- `resource_id`
- `resource_parent`
- `resource_name`

acl_privileges:

- `privilege_id`

- privilege_name

acl_rules:

- rule_id
- rule_role_id
- rule_resource_id
- rule_privilege_id
- rule_allow

Those are the four tables necessary for storing the ACL information. We are also going to add a fifth table that holds the actual API keys and a link for each key to a corresponding role:
acl_apikeys:

- apikey_key
- apikey_consumerid
- apikey_roleid

We could equally have added a one-to-many table allowing links between a single API key and multiple roles, but in our examples we will stick with the one-role-per-API-key rule. In a production application, the `apikey_consumerid` would link to a table holding contact or other relevant data for that API consumer.

Please note that you can create the tables mentioned here using the `zfws-acl.sql` script found in the `scripts/` directory. Add them using the command line MySQL client like this:

```
mysql -u zfws -p zfws < zfws-acl.sql
```

You should enter **zfws** as the password, if you have not changed that since reading Chapter 2.

The roles and resources we have discussed so far were provided merely as examples to help explain the concepts involved in Zend_Acl. It is therefore time for us to return to the data and requirements laid out in Chapter 2, where we identified the types of users for whom the web service is being created.

These included online web shops ran by partners, who want to be able to:

- check approximate stock figures
- place backorders
- fetch images for products

We create the role "partner" for them. Retail stores and chains want to:

- have all of the above
- place, update and remove orders
- check order status

We create the role "wholesale partner" for them. For the MTA web shop, we want:

- all of the above
- the ability to retrieve invoices
- a method for calculating order shipping costs

The role "webshop" is created for this. We are also going to add a few additional roles for our own convenience, such as the "anonymous" role, a more general "customer" role for API consumers, who are permitted to create an order, and finally the "admin" role.

The final set of rules we defined is represented in the following matrices, and they reflect the rules entered in the database (see `http://zfws/acltest2.php`). The following table represents the access restrictions on different parts of the application:

```
+--------------------+-----+-----+-----+
|                    |API  |data |admin|
+--------------------+-----+-----+-----+
|anonymous           |     |     |     |
+--------------------+-----+-----+-----+
|customer            |x    |x    |     |
+--------------------+-----+-----+-----+
|admin               |x    |x    |x    |
+--------------------+-----+-----+-----+
|partner             |x    |x    |     |
+--------------------+-----+-----+-----+
|wholesale partner   |x    |x    |     |
+--------------------+-----+-----+-----+
|webshop             |x    |x    |     |
+--------------------+-----+-----+-----+
```

Here we see which role has access to what kind of web service:

```
+--------------------+--------+--------+--------+--------+
|                    |soap    |rest    |xmlrpc  |jsonrpc |
+--------------------+--------+--------+--------+--------+
|anonymous           |        |        |        |        |
+--------------------+--------+--------+--------+--------+
|customer            |x       |x       |        |        |
+--------------------+--------+--------+--------+--------+
|admin               |x       |x       |x       |x       |
+--------------------+--------+--------+--------+--------+
|partner             |x       |x       |x       |x       |
+--------------------+--------+--------+--------+--------+
|wholesale partner   |x       |x       |x       |x       |
+--------------------+--------+--------+--------+--------+
|webshop             |x       |x       |x       |x       |
+--------------------+--------+--------+--------+--------+
```

Finally, we see the order and invoice objects which are exposed through various parts of our web services, and what kind of access is allowed for the different roles:

```
+--------------------+--------+----+------+------+--------+----+------+------+
|                    |orders  |    |      |      |invoices|    |      |      |
+--------------------+--------+----+------+------+--------+----+------+------+
|                    |create  |read|update|delete|create  |read|update|delete|
+--------------------+--------+----+------+------+--------+----+------+------+
|anonymous           |        |    |      |      |        |    |      |      |
```

```
+-------------------+--------+----+------+------+--------+----+------+------+
|customer           |x       |    |      |      |        |    |      |      |
+-------------------+--------+----+------+------+--------+----+------+------+
|admin              |        |    |      |      |        |    |      |      |
+-------------------+--------+----+------+------+--------+----+------+------+
|partner            |x       |x   |      |      |        |    |      |      |
+-------------------+--------+----+------+------+--------+----+------+------+
|wholesale partner  |x       |x   |x     |x     |        |    |      |      |
+-------------------+--------+----+------+------+--------+----+------+------+
|webshop            |x       |x   |x     |x     |x       |x   |      |      |
+-------------------+--------+----+------+------+--------+----+------+------+
```

Browsing `http://zfws/acltest2.php` will show the entire table, with additional columns for products, stock and shipping.

This information was created on the fly from the information stored in the database and used to set up a `Zend_Acl` object. It gives an up-to-date overview of all rules set. This information could be valuable for your customers too, to show on their personal account page for example where they can check for themselves what type of rights are assigned to them.

Just for your information, the tables were created using `Zend_Text_Table`. See the code for `acltest2.php` and the reference manual for more details on the `Zend_Text` component if you are interested.

Now we reconstruct the `Zend_Acl` object using the information from the database. This should be reasonably easy to understand. Every part is loaded from the database and added to the `Zend_Acl` object in the correct order:

```
$acl = new Zend_Acl();
$roles = $db->fetchAssoc('select * from acl_roles');
foreach ($roles as $role) {
   $acl->addRole($role['role_name']);
}

$resources = $db->fetchAssoc('select * from acl_resources ORDER BY
    resource_parent ASC');

foreach ($resources as $resource) {
   $resource_parent = NULL;
   if (!empty($resource['resource_parent']) && isset($resources[$resource['
       resource_parent']])) {
      $parent_id = $resource['resource_parent'];
      $resource_parent = $resources[$parent_id]['resource_name'];
```

```
    }
       $acl->addResource($resource['resource_name'], $resource_parent);
    }

    $privileges = $db->fetchPairs('select privilege_id,privilege_name ' .
                                  ' from acl_privileges');

    $rules = $db->fetchAssoc('select * from acl_rules');

    foreach($rules as $rule) {
       $privilege = NULL;
       if (isset($privileges[$rule['rule_privilege_id']])) {
          $privilege = $privileges[$rule['rule_privilege_id']];
       }
       $role = NULL;
       if (isset($roles[$rule['rule_role_id']])) {
          $role = $roles[$rule['rule_role_id']]['role_name'];
       }
       $resource = NULL;
       if (isset($resources[$rule['rule_resource_id']])) {
          $resource = $resources[$rule['rule_resource_id']]['resource_name'];
       }

       if ($rule['rule_allow'] > 0) {
          $acl->allow($role, $resource, $privilege);
       } else {
          $acl->deny($role, $resource, $privilege);
       }
    }
}
```

Just one final warning before moving to the next paragraphs: the way we stored our ACL information is probably not the most foolproof. As soon as you start inheriting from other roles, you will have to adapt the code and tables accordingly. Before you start using Zend_Acl in your own project, take your time to design your own implementation the way you need it for **your** project. The above method of storing a tree-like structure for the resources is very basic. For more complex trees, you should consider another approach like the one explained at the MySQL site[1].

Note, these keys were added and can be used for testing:

key   role

---
[1] http://dev.mysql.com/tech-resources/articles/hierarchical-data.html

```
cuo4sohD      webshop
fihaig2I      wholesale partner
in4Gah3T      admin
oon4Choh      partner
yoh7Ixoh      customer
```

How to Use Zend_Acl in our Web Service Code

How are we going to pull this information from the database and make it available to the rest of our application? A new class, `Mta_Access`, will instantiate `Zend_Acl`, load everything necessary from the tables in the database, and also create the ACL object. The new class is as follows:

```
class Mta_Access
{
   private $_db     = NULL;
   private $_acl    = NULL;
   private $_key    = false;
   private $_rpcmap = NULL;

   public function __construct($db = NULL)
   {
      if ($db) {
         $this->setDb($db);
         $this->_createAcl();
      }
   }

   public function setDb($db)
   {
      if (isset($db) && ($db instanceof Zend_Db_Adapter_Abstract) ) {
         $this->_db = $db;
      }
   }

   private function _createAcl()
   {
      $this->_acl = new Zend_Acl();

      // ... information is added to the ACL object like we did in the previous
         example
```

```
    }
    public function getAcl()
    {
        if (!isset($this->_acl)) {
            $this->_createAcl();
        }
        return $this->_acl;
    }
}
```

This creates the ACL object as an internal property which can be retrieved using `getAcl()`. Some additional functionality is going to be added. The `getKeyRole()` method will do a lookup to check if a given key has a role associated with it.

```
public function getKeyRole($key = '')
{
    $query = 'SELECT r.role_name FROM acl_roles AS r LEFT JOIN acl_apikeys AS
        k
            ON r.role_id = k.apikey_role_id
            WHERE k.apikey_key = ? and k.apikey_role_id IS NOT NULL';
    return $this->_db->fetchOne($query, $key);
}
```

If no match is found, the "anonymous" role can be applied, leaving the initiator of the call to the web service with very limited access to the web services. An extra table in the database will link methods to resources and privileges. The table `acl_methods` has these columns:

- method_name
- method_resource_id
- method_privilege_id

This maps methods to a resource and a privilege. For ease of use, we also added `methodAllowed()`, which takes a method name and checks if access is allowed:

```
public function methodAllowed($method = '', $service = 'soap')
{
```

166 ■ Limiting Access using Zend_Acl

```php
      if (!isset($this->_acl)) {
         $this->_createAcl();
      }
      if ($this->_key  && !empty($method)) {
         $role = $this->getKeyRole($this->_key);
         if (!empty($role) && $this->_acl->isAllowed($role, $service, 'use')) {
            $params = $this->_getMethodInfo(strtolower($method));
            if (is_array($params)) {
               return $this->_acl->isAllowed($role,
                                             $params['resource_name'],
                                             $params['privilege_name']);
            }
         }
      }
      return false;
   }

   private function _getMethodInfo($method = '')
   {
      if (!isset($this->_rpcmap)) {
         $this->_getAllMethodInfo();
      }
      if (isset($this->_rpcmap[$method])) {
         return $this->_rpcmap[$method];
      }
      return false;
   }

   private function _getAllMethodInfo()
   {
      $query = 'SELECT m.method_name, r.resource_name,p.privilege_name
                FROM acl_methods m LEFT JOIN acl_resources r ON
                m.method_resource_id = r.resource_id LEFT JOIN
                acl_privileges p ON m.method_privilege_id = p.privilege_id
                WHERE r.resource_id IS NOT NULL AND p.privilege_id IS NOT
                NULL';
      $this->_rpcmap = $this->_db->fetchAssoc($query);
      // this property would be an interesting candidate for being cached...
   }

   public function setKey($key = '')
   {
      $this->_key = $key;
   }
```

Each RPC-style method should be linked to a resource and privilege, which will keep our ACL matrix clean and straightforward. A simple usage example will clear things up a bit:

```
$access = new Mta_Access();
$access->setKey($apikey);
$access->methodAllowed('getStockFigures', 'soap');
```

In our class this will result in:

- the private property $_apikey being set
- methodAllowed() being called, inside the role for the API key will be retrieved
- the role will be checked for being allowed to use the "soap" resource
- the method's role and privilege will be retrieved using _getMethodInfo() and an internal map which is created using _ getAllMethodInfo()
- finally the role will be checked for being allowed to use the mentioned privilege on the associated resource for the RPC method being called initially

Note that we could similarly have defined each RPC-style method as a resource, with a privilege of "use". Here we chose to map them to a certain resource and privilege however, as this seemed an interesting approach to keep the ACL matrices clean and simple.

The Mta_Access object, once created, can be stored in the registry for example which makes it available to other parts of our code.

Add Checks to Existing Services

The final step, adding the checks for the defined rules to our existing web service code, is actually quite simple. We will handle the services one by one.

SOAP

In the existing SOAP server classes `Mta_Soap_Server` and `Mta_Servicewrapper` we created in previous chapters, we can change the existing `_hasAccess()` method and incorporate some ACL checks:

```
protected function _hasAccess($apikey, $method)
{
    // if apikey has no access, return false
    if (Zend_Registry::isRegistered('Mta_Access')) {

        $access = Zend_Registry::get('Mta_Access');
        $access->setKey($apikey);
        return $access->methodAllowed($method);
    }

    // else
    return false;
}
```

Now calling `getOrderStatus()`, using for example "oon4Choh" as the API key (associated with the 'partner' role) will allow for retrieving the status of the order ("shipped"). Calling with a non-existent key or a key with insufficient rights will result in an "access denied" response.

REST

Our customized REST service resides inside `Rest_Controller`-derived controllers. Making `Mta_Access` available to that code can be done using an extra Bootstrap method, `_initAccess()`. We create the `Zend_Acl` object using `Mta_Access` and place it in the registry:

```
protected function _initAccess()
{
    $this->bootstrap('db');
    $db = $this->getResource('db');

    $access = new Mta_Access();
    $access->setDb($db);
    Zend_Registry::set('Mta_Access', $access);
```

        }

Now we can update the _hasAccess() method in the Mta_Rest_Controller:

```
protected function _hasAccess($apikey, $resource, $action)
{
   if (Zend_Registry::isRegistered('Mta_Access')) {
      $access = Zend_Registry::get('Mta_Access');
      $role = $access->getKeyRole($apikey);
      if (empty($role)) {
         return false;
      }
      $acl = $access->getAcl();
      if ($acl->isAllowed($role, 'rest', 'use')) {
         $priv = NULL;
         switch($action) {
            case 'post':
               $priv = 'create';
               break;
            case 'index':
            case 'get':
               $priv = 'read';
               break;
            case 'put':
               $priv = 'update';
               break;
            case 'delete':
               $priv = 'delete';
               break;
         }

          if ($acl->isAllowed($role, $resource, $priv)) {
             return true;
          }
       }
   }
   return false;
}
```

We map the HTTP POST, GET, PUT and DELETE actions to the privileges used in our ACL solution. A call to http://zfws/rest/orders/apikey/oon4Choh will now result in valid data; leaving the API key out will show an "access denied" result.

XML-RPC

Also in our customized XML-RPC server in XMLRPCbis.php, some lines are added in order to check for access to the requested method:

```php
$access = new Mta_Access();
$db = $application->getBootstrap()->getResource('db');
$access->setDb($db);

Zend_Registry::set('Mta_Access', $access);

$data = file_get_contents('php://input');
$dom = new DOMDocument();

if (!$dom->loadXML((string) $data)) {
   echo $server->fault('Invalid XML', 400);
} else {
   $xml = simplexml_load_string((string) $data);
   if (isset($xml->methodName)
     && isset($xml->params) && isset($xml->params->param[0])) {

      if (Zend_Registry::isRegistered('Mta_Access')) {
         $access = Zend_Registry::get('Mta_Access');
         $access->setKey($xml->params->param[0]->value);
         $method = strtolower(str_replace('zfws.', '', $xml->methodName));
         if ($access->methodAllowed($method,'xmlrpc')) {
            //then strip it out
            unset($xml->params->param[0]);
            $xmlstring = (string) $xml->asXml();

            //remove whitespace and empty lines
            $xmlstring = trim($xmlstring);
            $xmlstring = preg_replace("/(^[\r\n]*|[\r\n]+)[\s\t]*[\r\n]+/",
                                   "\n", $xmlstring);

            $request = new Zend_XmlRpc_Request();
            $request->loadXml($xmlstring);
            echo $server->handle($request);
         } else {
            echo $server->fault('Access not allowed', 403);
         }

      } else {
         echo $server->fault('Error during access control', 500);
      }
```

```
    } else {
       echo $server->fault('Missing API key', 403);
    }
}
```

The API key is read from the first parameter received, and access is checked similarly to how it was done in the SOAP server code. If access is granted, the API key is removed from the parameters, whitespace is removed and the request XML is passed to the actual server. Also note the second argument to `methodAllowed()`. This will result in an additional check being done for the key to be able to use the XML-RPC interface.

JSON-RPC

Changes to the code in our existing file `JSONRPCtris.php` are very similar to the API key checks introduced in the XML-RPC code:

```
$access = new Mta_Access();
$db = $application->getBootstrap()->getResource('db');
$access->setDb($db);

Zend_Registry::set('Mta_Access',$access);

$server = new Zend_Json_Server();
Zend_Loader::loadClass('Mta_Service');
$server->setClass('MTA_Service');

$request = new Zend_Json_Server_Request_Http();
$params = $request->getParams();
if (isset($params[0]) && isset($params[0]['apikey'])) {
   // check access for key
   if (Zend_Registry::isRegistered('Mta_Access')) {
      $method = strtolower($request->getMethod());
      $access = Zend_Registry::get('Mta_Access');
      $access->setKey($params[0]['apikey']);
      if ($access->methodAllowed($method, 'jsonrpc')) {
         $request->setParams($params[1]);
      } else {
         $server->fault('Not allowed', '',
                     'API key ' . $params[0]['apikey'] . ' not allowed');
      }
```

```
    } else {
       $server->fault('Access control error','',
                    'error encountered during ACL check');
    }
} else {
   $server->fault('Not allowed', '', 'API key missing');
}

$server->setAutoEmitResponse(false);
$response = $server->handle($request);

echo $response;
```

The API key is checked and removed from the parameters if access is granted. The resulting request is then passed on to the actual server.

Each time we only added a few lines of code in a central location, for every web service created before. We are able to reuse the same set of ACL rules and our newly created `Mta_Access` class, without too much manipulation of the existing code.

Summary

- We explored `Zend_Acl` and how to apply it to existing code
- We created a database backend for the `Zend_Acl` roles, rules, resources and privileges

Deliverables:

- The hardcoded API keys are replaced by real checks for rules defined in a flexible way in the database. We could even create a web-based interface for MTA so they could be able to manage the ACL themselves, if they wish.

Chapter 9

Performance and Scaling

Introduction

Making a web service scale, tracing and solving performance bottlenecks, and designing fault-tolerant and high availability web server infrastructure is something of an art in itself. A thorough treatment of the subject could fill a full shelf of books, so do not expect this chapter to solve all performance problems. We will list a few tips, tools and examples that can help you in your search of a solution for handling a boom in traffic or a steep fall in performance. You will not find a lot of example code in this chapter however, unlike previous chapters.

Where to Search

Whenever you are trying to pinpoint the reason for bottlenecks or slowdowns, you should take a look at different layers of your application and infrastructure. A cause of the troubles, or multiple causes, can be situated in any of these:

Network

A limited uplink to the Internet or troubles in an upstream network can be the cause of your issues. A broken switch, badly configured router or firewall, faulty cables, nearly anything is possible.

If you use multiple servers such as a frontend application server and a back-end database server, do not forget to have a look at how they are interconnected too. Adding a separate high-speed network for server-to-server communication can solve some issues right away.

Server Hardware and Tiered Setup

Is the hardware used for the server sufficient? Do all components in the machine work as expected? Some issues such as a failing hard disk can be caught by monitoring, others will only be revealed when it is already too late. Cooling and a sufficient, stable power supply are important too, of course.

Adding memory and processors to an existing machine or machines is called *scaling up* or *vertical scaling*. Adding *more machines* is called *scaling out* or *horizontal scaling* as you are adding more of the same machines in a certain layer of your architecture. For example, if you have two frontend servers answering to the same domain name, and DNS points to both of them, you can easily scale out by adding one or two more of the same machines. It will distribute load and is often seen in a tiered web hosting environment as a better, and sometimes cheaper, solution. A major database server with big indexes in memory might benefit from scaling up on the other hand, by just plugging in more memory.

If you wonder what a tiered setup is, basically it just means that different tasks are assigned to different layers of servers. A typical two-tier setup having:

- database server(s)
- frontend web server(s)

can be turned into a three-tiered setup, by adding a layer:

- database server(s)
- caching server(s) or caching layer
- frontend web server(s)

The frontend web servers now call a caching layer (web services with caching of data on Memcached servers for example) first and if nothing is in the cache, the web service can talk to the database backend servers. Here it is interesting to see that web services are used in a scaling setup to further spread the load and efficiently use a caching layer. Indeed, web services themselves can be used when designing your infrastructure for high performance.

We can go a bit further and add a fourth layer in front, having some reverse proxies caching static data:

- database server(s)
- caching server(s) or caching layer
- frontend web server(s)
- reverse proxy layer

The frontend web servers in this case typically do not point images, JavaScript and CSS files to the frontend web server's URLs like `http://www.example.com/css/somefile.css`. Instead they use something like `http://static.example.com/css/somefile.css` which is directed by DNS to the reverse proxy servers. These will, upon receiving the request for `css/somefile.css` check whether they have the file in cache, and if this is not the case, fetch it from the upstream frontend web servers, then place it into their cache store and return the output to the browser.

In the case of a web service, this could be used to serve the WSDL files for a SOAP server, or SMD files for a JSON-RPC service, for example.

Many variations on an N-tiered setup are possible: most of the time your setup will start small and eventually evolve with the intention of keeping up with the popularity of the application, site or service you are building or supporting. Just make sure that the code you write is able to handle this kind of scaling out and layering.

Note that cloud-based computing can offer a solution too, offering you the ability to scale up by adding more memory to your cloud-based server or by allowing you to quickly setup additional server images and thus scale horizontally.

Operating System

Is the operating system in use on the servers the most efficient? Is it tuned by an expert? Is it actually capable of handling the hardware it is running on? Does it have known driver issues? Is it actually the best solution available?

Some operating systems are prone to viruses and bot scripts which may cause a slowdown without bringing the machine to a real halt. It is not always easy to detect these kinds of parasites, let alone to remove them without trace.

It is hard to write something about operating systems and PHP support without starting a holy war on why a specific version is superior, so I just leave it to the reader to choose, since I am probably biased too. Have a look around on the Internet and see what the big players are using; they probably made a well thought-out choice.

Web Server

Does the web server software in use offer the best possible solution available for powering your particular application or web service? Apache for example is in widespread use, and is stable and well-documented. Tuning it is often overlooked, however, and default installations frequently have many modules and features enabled which are not all necessary for your application. Unload or remove Apache modules that are not in use by your application, and tune some of the Apache configuration settings as suggested in the Apache manual[1].

A simple trick for speeding up Apache, is moving the mod_rewrite rules found in .htaccess to the VirtualHost definition:

```
<VirtualHost *:80>
    ServerAdmin you@example.com
    ServerName zfws
    DocumentRoot /web/zfws/public
    <Directory />
        AllowOverride None
    </Directory>
    <Directory /web/zfws/public>
        Options Indexes FollowSymLinks MultiViews
        AllowOverride None
        #start copy from .htaccess
```

---
[1] http://httpd.apache.org/docs/2.0/misc/perf-tuning.html

```
        RewriteEngine On
        RewriteRule ^SOAP(/?)$ SOAP.php?v=1.0 [NC,L]
        RewriteRule ^v([0-9]+).([0-9]+)/SOAP(/?)$ SOAP.php?v=$1.$2 [NC,L]
        RewriteCond %{REQUEST_FILENAME} -s [OR]
        RewriteCond %{REQUEST_FILENAME} -l [OR]
        RewriteCond %{REQUEST_FILENAME} -d
        RewriteRule ^.*$ - [NC,L]
        RewriteRule ^.*$ index.php [NC,L]
        #stop copy from .htaccess
        Order allow,deny
        allow from all
    </Directory>
    setenv APPLICATION_ENV development
    LogLevel warn
    ErrorLog /var/log/apache2/zfws-error.log
    CustomLog /var/log/apache2/zfws-access.log combined
</VirtualHost>
```

Inside the `Directory` container, the `AllowOverride All` directive was changed to `AllowOverride None`, and this does the trick. No .htaccess files will be parsed, and this will result in far less disk accesses by the web server.

Lightweight alternatives for Apache like lighttpd (often pronounced "lighty") and Nginx have gained some ground over the last few years, and are worth a look if you are considering your options.

Database

MySQL, despite some criticism, can power large and complex databases, but configuring it correctly is often overlooked. There exist a few off-the-shelf solutions that can provide you with useful tips for your setup: the MySQL Tuning Primer[2] and MySQLTuner[3] inspect your running server and the output hints at possible changes in the configuration.

Slow query logging can help you find the worst performing queries. The online MySQL manual[4] explains how to activate slow query logging and points to a tool called `mysqldumpslow` that can help you in analyzing the slow query log.

---

[2] http://forge.mysql.com/projects/project.php?id=44
[3] http://www.mysqltuner.pl
[4] http://dev.mysql.com/doc/refman/5.1/en/slow-query-log.html

Do not forget to turn slow query logging off after a while, as the log file can grow in size very quickly indeed. Troublesome queries identified using slow query analysis can be further examined using the EXPLAIN statement[5].

An often-used trick is splitting the queries based on whether they are read or write queries. In situations where MySQL is running in a master-slave setup, where data written to the master is replicated to the slave, a tool like MySQL Proxy is able to send SELECT queries to a MySQL slave server while INSERT, UPDATE and DELETE queries are sent to the master server. MySQL Proxy can be run as a daemon on a separate server or on the frontend application servers and can listen on the usual port 3306. It can load custom scripts written in Lua, and one of the sample scripts that comes with the source allows for checking and sending each query to the appropriate hostname. The application connecting to the MySQL database does not need big changes; it simply needs to connect to MySQL Proxy just as it would connect to a regular MySQL server.

As a last possible measure, you can consider alternatives for MySQL too of course, like Drizzle, PostgreSQL or SQLite.

Code

Last but not least, poorly designed or inefficient code can bring a site to its knees before you can even start to consider one of the above points. Zend Framework itself includes a large number of files, and performance tuning it is a hot topic in the developer community. In fact, version 2.0 will already address some of these issues. In case you need some pointers, the Zend Framework manual[6] has a chapter on optimizing some of its parts.

Basic optimization of your setup can already be done using any of these techniques:

- By adding an opcode cache like APC, Xcache, Zend Optimizer or eAccelerator for example. Opcode caches cache the compiled source code (the "opcodes"), and this saves some disk seeks and processing cycles on subsequent requests. Some of them add optimization tricks to handle the code more efficiently. In a lot of cases this provides sufficient gains in performance.

---

[5] http://dev.mysql.com/doc/refman/5.1/en/using-explain.html
[6] http://framework.zend.com/manual/en/performance.html

- By placing the code on a RAM disk and serving it from that location might help too

- By using a static web server or reverse proxy like Squid or Varnish

- By using caching where possible, and avoid unnecessary database or web service queries. Some caching examples using Zend_Acl will follow in the next paragraphs

- By fixing your code

Read your code, be critical of your own work, test it and optimize it. Benchmarks are your best friend once you start performance tuning. You can find a lot of information on the Internet about how a certain approach is faster then another one, such as preferring the use of single rather than double quotes for quoting strings, since PHP looks for variables to interpret inside double quotes.

Do exercise caution, however: some of these "micro optimization" tips out there are worthwhile, but others are just that: micro optimizations. One of the best, and often forgotten, tips is to avoid writing your own solutions if there is a PHP function that fills your need. Check the manual, as there are hundreds and hundreds of functions, and there are countless extensions adding even more. These are implemented in C and 99% of the time they are faster than you could possibly achieve by writing your own solution mimicking their functionality.

How to Detect Bottlenecks

Detecting bottlenecks and degraded performance can be done by monitoring every aspect of the infrastructure involved, by analyzing the code and by using benchmarks when trying some optimization tricks.

Monitoring Tools

There is a wide variety of monitoring tools for hardware and network resources, from the commercial ones to open source tools like monit, Zabbix and Nagios/Icinga.

There are also commercial services promising to measure your service response times every few minutes and to warn you when performance degrades.

Measurement and Benchmarks

A few benchmarking tools exist. ApacheBench or ab is often used for testing the requests per second a website or application can handle. A typical output for an ab test is as follows:

```
$ ab -c 5 -n 500 http://zfws/rest/orders/
Benchmarking zfws (be patient)
Completed 100 requests
...
Finished 500 requests

Server Software:        Apache/2.2.12
Server Hostname:        zfws
Server Port:            80
Document Path:          /rest/orders/
Document Length:        221 bytes

Concurrency Level:      5
Time taken for tests:   19.285 seconds
Complete requests:      500
Failed requests:        0
Write errors:           0
Total transferred:      202500 bytes
HTML transferred:       110500 bytes
Requests per second:    25.93 [#/sec] (mean)
Time per request:       192.846 [ms] (mean)
Time per request:       38.569 [ms] (mean, across all concurrent requests)
Transfer rate:          10.25 [Kbytes/sec] received

Connection Times (ms)
              min  mean[+/-sd] median   max
Connect:        0    0   0.0      0       0
Processing:    58  192  62.6    192     401
Waiting:       58  192  62.8    189     401
Total:         58  192  62.6    192     401

Percentage of the requests served within a certain time (ms)
  50%    192
  ...
 100%    401 (longest request)
```

Here, we sent five hundred page requests, including up to five concurrent ones to our REST controller, which returns information on registered orders. One of the most interesting and often quoted results is the requests per second an application or website is able to handle (in this case 25.93). This single number is often used to compare results between benchmarks.

What you should do once you start tuning, is record a few of these basic benchmarking tests to start with. These will be your baseline values to compare to each time an optimization measure is taken. We will repeat the above test once we have some caching added to the REST service.

Siege is an alternative to `ab`, and tools like JMeter and Grinder allow for testing more complex site visitor patterns and the corresponding response times.

Detecting Code Issues

Detecting potential hotspots for trouble in your code can become a lot easier if you use a combination of Valgrind and Xdebug to profile your code for example.

To give you a hint on what kind of output you may expect from these tools, have a look at Figure 9.1.

Figure 9.1

As you can see, this combination of tools will give you a visual impression of the amount of time spent while executing various parts of your code. In this image, only a part of the so-called Callee map is shown. The Callee map compares individual parts of your code being called to the overall footprint. It also displays a list of executed calls, memory used and time spent (not shown in our image). You can drill down further to identify parts of your code that take an unreasonable amount of execution time or unreasonable amounts of memory. So this tool allows us to identify parts of the code which could cause trouble, now or later.

The output used for creating a report like the above is logged by the PHP extension Xdebug and can be read and displayed by one of the Valgrind tools. On Linux you can use Kcachegrind, on Windows you have WinCachegrind at your disposal.

Making Xdebug log the profiling logs is done by adding these configuration options (inside `/etc/php5/conf.d/xdebug.ini` for example) to PHP's ini settings:

```
zend_extension=/usr/lib/php5/20060613+lfs/xdebug.so
xdebug.profiler_enable = 1
xdebug.profiler_output_dir = /tmp
```

Installing the Xdebug extension depends on your operating system, on Ubuntu you can just execute `apt-get install php5-xdebug`. On Windows, if you used XAMPP as suggested, Xdebug is included but you just need to uncomment this line in `php.ini`:

```
;zend_extension = "\xampp\php\ext\php_xdebug.dll"
```

Further down the `php.ini` file you can add the lines enabling the profiler and designating the output directory for the log files.

Point your browser at `http://zfws/rest/orders` and a new file will be written in the defined output directory, which looks like `cachegrind.out.<int>`. You can load this file using Kcachegrind or WinCachegrind, the result will look like our example image. More information on Valgrind can be found at the official website[7].

Add Some Caching

Caching of data in our application or web service is relatively easy to add and will add significant speed gains.

---

[7] http://valgrind.org

Zend Framework has the Zend_Cache component, which supports different cache backends. Among these we have Memcached, available on your system if you followed the guidelines in Appendix A. Memcached is a key-value database, storing its data in volatile memory, specifically RAM. PHP has the memcache extension which allows us to talk to Memcached using its native protocol.

We are going to add some caching support and to do so we are going to add some code to our `Bootstrap.php` file again:

```
protected function _initCache()
{
   $frontendOptions = array(
      'automatic_serialization' => true,
      'lifetime' => 9800 // 3 hours
   );

   $backendOptions = array(
      'servers' => array(
                  array('host' => 'localhost',
                        'port' => 11211,
                        'persistent' => 1
                     )
                  )
   );

   $cache = Zend_Cache::factory('Core',
                              'Zend_Cache_Backend_Memcached',
                              $frontendOptions,
                              $backendOptions,
                              false,
                              true);

   Zend_Registry::set('Zend_Cache', $cache);
}
```

Without going into too much detail, this creates a `Zend_Cache` object using Memcached as the backend for cache storage. The cache object is made available using the registry, and cached data is considered valid for three hours.

In `Rest_OrdersController` for example we could now add:

```
public function indexAction()
{
```

186 ■ Performance and Scaling

```
    $cache = Zend_Registry::get('Zend_Cache');
    if (!$result = $cache->load('get_orders')) {
        $order = new Mta_Model_Order();
        $result = $order->fetchAll();
        $cache->save($result, 'get_orders_');
    }
    $this->_createResponse(200, $result);
}
```

If a cached value with the key "get_orders" is found, that value is returned, otherwise the data is fetched from the database, written to cache and returned. Next time a call is issued towards http://zfws/rest/orders, the cached value will be returned.

Now you should repeat the small ab-based benchmark test we did before. In our case, the number or requests being handled per second increased to 32.48 from 25.93. That's a good improvement, and this should continue to improve when caching larger datasets throughout the different web services.

Suppose you want the orders to be updated once there is a change, waiting for three hours might be too long for some customers to see a change there. The solution for this is to modify the postAction() method, where new orders are created:

```
public function postAction()
{
    if ($this->_cache) {
        $this->_cache->remove('get_orders');
    }
    // handle the creation of the order here
    // ...
}
```

When a new order is created, the cached value with the key "get_orders" is cleaned. The next call to http://zfws/rest/orders will seed the cache with a new result set from the database. The subsequent call will result in a cache hit and the database will not be queried.

Other candidates for caching might include:

- the WSDL file being generated for our SOAP service

- the result sets from certain RPC methods in Mta_Service that just fetch information from the database

- the ACL object and the array mapping RPC methods to resources and privileges in the previous chapter (in the `Mta_Access` class)

As you may have noticed, naming the keys consistently becomes quite important. Suppose you have an order created through the SOAP service method `createOrder()`, then the same cached object with a key "get_orders" should be cleared by that method. Otherwise, the REST interface users would be stuck with stale data. So the same keys should be used consistently wherever the same data is being handled.

As a side note, adding this to our `_initCache()` method in `Bootstrap.php`:

```
Zend_Db_Table_Abstract::setDefaultMetadataCache($cache);
```

will allow `Zend_Db_Table` to store some of the metadata it reads from each table into the cache backend. This too will result in increased performance, since otherwise `Zend_Db_Table` will have to fetch this metadata each time from the database.

Summary

- We have some insights on how to start optimizing and scaling our web service
- We touched on some basic Zend_Cache usage with Memcached storage and applied it successfully to existing code
- Caching keys should be named following a convention

Deliverables:

- Basic example code for adding caching to the web services was tested with success.

Chapter 10

Unit Testing

Introduction and Background

Unit testing is a method for testing code, or pieces of code to see if the code responds as expected under given conditions. Testing is done on the smallest possible testable piece of code. The smallest piece possible could mean a certain piece in the flow, an object or class or even just a single function or method. In ideal circumstances, tests should be able to run separately, although multiple tests can be run in a suite or group of tests which allows for testing more overall functionality.

Unit tests are a useful tool for detecting changes in pieces of code in one location that could affect the behavior and output of an application in another, related part. When doing testing only manually, it is sometimes hard to find and predict all possible effects. Automated unit testing allows for quickly testing broad parts of an application. Consider this scenario:

- a web service is created, returning product information from a database

- a unit test that requests product information for a random product is created and checks the format of the returned information

At a certain point in time, product information for some products is to be fetched from a second database too, and as a developer you have to add the lookup functionality in the web service. The resulting output should be exactly the same as the output created for products stored in the first database:

- new code is added, doing a lookup in the second database if the first one returns no result
- the unit test is run to see if the output is in the appropriate format

If you are a single developer on a project, you may see the above as unnecessary and too much effort for just a limited extra bonus. Unit tests may indeed take some of your precious time. Creating the additional code and just hand-testing it once you are done may seem to be faster than creating a unit test. Unit tests however allow for re-running tests afterward with just a single command and eventually will help save time instead.

In situations where you are part of a team of multiple developers working on different parts of the code, unit tests may allow you to test part of the code you have no knowledge of, making you feel comfortable with changes *you* may have made. Suppose that 80% of the functionality is covered by unit tests and some developer changes a piece of a core library that affects output in a location he just forgot to test manually. The odds are high that the change is detected by the tests covering the affected area, as some may fail. In this way, you are far more likely to identify and fix problems *before* they are reported back to you as a bug or error.

As you can see, this will ultimately lead to a piece of code or an application that nearly always behaves as expected, and less unexpected behavior and bugs will be filed by end users. This is of course much appreciated by the people actually paying for the end result.

In a larger project, unit tests are typically run automatically at certain intervals of time or, if continuous builds are created, on each build. The results of these tests are used to keep the code consistent, and should a unit test fail, the code or test will be fixed as soon as possible.

Note that you can find more on continuous integration and continuous builds at Wikipedia[1]. PHP's ecosystem has tools that will facilitate the setup of continuous build services like Xinc, phpUnderControl or Hudson. There is also Arbit which is still in beta, but promises to become a contender soon.

---

[1] http://en.wikipedia.org/wiki/Continuous_integration

Enter PHPUnit

Zend Framework has a testing component, Zend_Test. It is mostly aimed at testing the MVC parts of an application and is based on PHPUnit[2]. PHPUnit is a well documented and very mature framework for building and running unit tests. If you followed the guidelines for setting up your development environment in Appendix A, you should have PHPUnit ready for use on your workstation. You can test to see if it works by trying the following on the command line. This will tell you the version of PHPUnit installed on your system:

```
zfws@zfws:/web/zfws$ phpunit --version
PHPUnit 3.4.12 by Sebastian Bergmann.
```

Let us create a simple example, testing the someMathConstant() function we used for a few examples in previous chapters:

```
class ExampleOneTest extends PHPUnit_Framework_TestCase
{
    public function testSomeMathConstant()
    {
        $this->assertEquals('3.14159265', someMathConstant('pi'));
        $this->assertEquals('be rational', someMathConstant('e'));
        $this->assertEquals('unknown variable', someMathConstant(''));
    }
}
```

The code is available in tests/custom/exampleOneTest.php, and you can test it running the following command:

```
zfws@zfws:/web/zfws/tests$ phpunit custom/exampleOneTest.php
PHPUnit 3.4.12 by Sebastian Bergmann.
Time: 0 seconds, Memory: 8.50Mb
OK (1 test, 3 assertions)
```

We actually tested the behavior of the function when executed with different parameters. If someone changes the function, the unit test should continue to succeed,

---

[2] http://www.phpunit.de

since other code may depend on the three function calls we tested. If it does not, either the test or the code has to be changed.

As a member of the xUnit family of unit testing frameworks, PHPUnit follows a common approach, consisting of the elements following hereafter.

Test Fixtures

A test fixture, or "context", is the state of the system under test (SUT) a given test is supposed to start with. Suppose you want to test if the first order in the database entered is stored correctly, this means that the table of orders in the database should be empty before you can start this test. It is up to you to create such a precondition before you actually run the test. For other tests to be run afterwards, the database should be restored to its original state afterwards too, to make further tests possible for example.

Setting up and restoring the fixture is the task of the developer constructing the unit test.

Test Cases and Test Suites

The test case class is the basic class from which all unit tests will be derived. A collection of test cases using the same fixture is referred to as a test suite. Test suites can be run with a single command, and you should take care that the order in which they are run is not important. Each case should be able to be run on its own and should not depend on the output or data created in another test case.

Execution

Execution of a test follows the flow as depicted in the following example class:

```
class SampleTest extends PHPUnit_Framework_TestCase
{
    public function setUp()
    {
        // preparation
    }

    public function testSomething()
```

```
    {
        $this->assertTrue(true);
    }

    public function tearDown()
    {
        // cleanup
    }
}
```

The system under test (SUT) is prepared for the tests in `setUp()`, then all methods following the test* naming convention are automatically executed by PHPUnit, and eventual cleanup of the tested system is done in `tearDown()`.

The `setUp()` and `tearDown()` methods could for example setup the database used for testing and cleaning up the information inserted in the database afterwards.

Assertions

Assertions verify the expected behavior of the unit under test. PHPUnit has a number of built-in assertion methods:

- `assertEquals()`
- `assertFalse()`
- `assertType()`
- `assertArrayHasKey()`

There are many more, so for a complete list, have a look at the manual on the PHPUnit website[3].

These assertions are used to compare the output of a method or variable obtained through executing part of the code to their expected values.

---
[3] http://www.phpunit.de/manual/3.4/en/index.html

Mocks and Stubs

When a piece of code interacts with a remote system, such as a remote web service somewhere on the Internet, it is possible that the service is not available or reachable while doing tests. It is also possible that if we would connect to that remote system while testing, our test could create undesired data which cannot be removed without the help of a third party. Unit testing has the concept of Test Doubles to avoid this. These test doubles will behave as the actual system the code is intended to connect to.

Stubs are objects used to replace real objects the system under test depends on. They return or define predefined values and thus allow the system to act as it normally would, without for example really connecting to a remote web service.

Mock objects on the other hand are test doubles that verify if a certain method is called by the system under test. They act as an observer that checks if a call to an external component is done according to certain expectations. Optionally they return predefined values too, like stubs.

Mocks and stubs are related, and PHPUnit has the getMock() method for creating both, accepting a class name as parameter. This method can automatically generate an object based on said class, and the resulting object can act as a mock or stub. By default the methods of the class are replaced with dummies, returning NULL. The original methods are not called. The dummy methods can be configured to return a certain value when called.

All of this may seem a bit vague, so let's look at a simple example of both Test Doubles. Let us create a simple test case in tests/custom/exampleTwoTest.php, were we are going to create a stub for Mta_Service, the class we used for creating the RPC type services:

```
class ExampleTwoTest extends PHPUnit_Framework_TestCase
{
  public function testStubService()
  {
    // create a stub for the Mta_Service class
    $stub = $this->getMock('Mta_Service');

    // configure
    $stub->expects($this->any())
        ->method('getStockFigures')
```

```
                ->will($this->returnValue(10));

        // check assertions
        $this->assertType(PHPUnit_Framework_Constraint_IsType::TYPE_INT,
                          $stub->getStockFigures(1));

        $this->assertEquals(10, $stub->getStockFigures(1));
    }
}
```

What is happening here? First, the stub is created based on `Mta_Service` and we tell the stub that a call to `getStockFigures()` should return "10". Then we test to see if a call to `getStockFigures()` returns an integer, followed by a test to see if the result equals "10". The test result will be just fine when we execute the test case from the command line:

```
zfws@zfws:/web/zfws/tests$ phpunit custom/exampleTwoTest.php
...
Time: 0 seconds, Memory: 8.75Mb
OK (1 test, 3 assertions)
```

Now, let us add an example mock object. To be able to produce a meaningful example, we have to add a new method to `Mta_Service` first and adapt our `getStockFigures()` method a little:

```
class Mta_Service
{
    // ...

    public function __setModel($model, $classtype = NULL)
    {
        if (!isset($classtype)) {
            $classtype = get_class($model);
        }
        switch($classtype) {
            case 'Mta_Model_Product':
                $this->_product = $model;
            case 'Mta_Model_Order':
                $this->_order = $model;
            case 'Mta_Model_Stock':
                $this->_stock = $model;
```

```
            break;
      }
   }

   public function getStockFigures($product_id)
   {
      if ($product_id > 0) {
         if (!$this->_stock) {
            Zend_Loader::loadFile(APPLICATION_PATH . '/models/Stock.php');
            $this->_stock = new Mta_Model_Stock();
         }
         return $this->_stock->getAvailable($product_id);
      } else {
         throw new Mta_Exception('Product id must be greater than 0', '888');
      }
   }
   // ...
}
```

The new method `__setModel()` allows us to specify a `Zend_Db_Table`-based object to be used for talking to the database. The "__" prefix ensures that WSDL generation will not pick up and expose this method in the auto-generated WSDL file, even if this is a public method. In `getStockFigures()`, we added some additional lines of code to see if the `Mta_Model_Stock` object has been set before as class property, which is exactly what we will do in our unit test with the mock object we are creating. Have another look at `ExampleTestTwo`, were we can add another test method:

```
public function testMockService()
{
   // create a mock Mta_Model_Stock
   $mock = $this->getMock('Mta_Model_Stock', array('getAvailable'));

   // configure mock
   $mock->expects($this->once())
        ->method('getAvailable')
        ->with($this->equalTo('1'));

   // create an instance of Mta_Service
   $service = new Mta_Service();

   // pass the mock as Mta_Model_Stock
   $service->__setModel($mock, 'Mta_Model_Stock');
```

```
    $service->getStockFigures(1);
}
```

First, a mock object is created to be used instead of the actual Mta_Model_Stock object. Only the getAvailable() method is stubbed. Then, in the configuration part, we tell that we expect a single call to the getAvailable() method with a parameter equaling "1". The Mta_Service object is created, and our mock object is set as the object to be used in Mta_Service::getAvailable(). The call to $service->getStockFigures(1) will result in the assertions being tested as configured for our mock object, since the mock object is used in getStockFigures() instead of the actual Mta_Model_Stock object. The result:

```
zfws@uhu:/web/zfws/tests$ phpunit custom/exampleTwoTest.php
..
Time: 0 seconds, Memory: 8.75Mb
OK (2 tests, 4 assertions)
```

The above should give you an idea of what is possible. If you are new to unit testing, all this might be a bit overwhelming but once you get a handle on it you will soon start to enjoy writing unit tests and appreciate the advantages they offer in the long run.

If a substantial part of your application code is covered by unit tests, it will be of great help for example the day you decide to upgrade the Zend Framework library files. Running the unit tests after that and fixing some minor things could be achieved in hours instead of days of manual testing parts of the application.

We are going to add some more examples for our web services and create test cases for:

- a client call using the built-in web service mocking functionality provided by PHPUnit

- the code that instantiates the SOAP service and add a test call to that object

- the results received from a call to the REST server

Mocking Web Services Using PHPUnit

PHPUnit supplies us with a utility tool that allows us to create a mock object based on a WSDL file. Just point getMockFromWsdl() to a WSDL location and a ready-to-use mock object is created for you instantly:

```
class SOAPTest extends PHPUnit_Framework_TestCase
{
   public function testClientCall()
   {
       $clientMock = $this->getMockFromWsdl('http://zfws/SOAP.php?WSDL=1',
                                            'MTA');

       $result = '321';

       $clientMock->expects($this->any())
                  ->method('getStockFigures')
                  ->will($this->returnValue('321'));

       $this->assertEquals($result, $clientMock->getStockFigures('oon4Choh', 1));
   }
}
```

What we tested here is a call to a method mock object based on our WSDL file for the SOAP service we created earlier. The code is saved in tests/custom/SOAPtest.php and can be run from the command line.

Testing the SOAP Service Setup and a Basic Call

The following case further illustrates the power of PHPUnit, we are able to compare the structure of two DomDocument objects. These objects can be created using an expected XML SOAP envelope and the actual XML SOAP envelope received as the result from a request passed to the SOAP server's handle() method.

The code in the next listing allows us to test if the SOAP server is instantiated correctly and handles a request as expected:

```
public function testServerSetupAndHandle()
{
    $options = array('soap_version' => SOAP_1_2);
```

```
    $server = new Zend_Soap_Server('http://zfws/SOAPbis.php?WSDL=1',
                                    $options);
    $server->setClass('Mta_Servicewrapper');

    $request = <<<END
<soapenv:Envelope>
... full SOAP request envelope as taken from soapUI
</soapenv:Envelope>
END;

    $server->setReturnResponse(true);
    $result = $server->handle($request);

    $expected = <<<END
<SOAP-ENV:Envelope>
... full SOAP expected response envelope as taken from soapUI
</SOAP-ENV:Envelope>
END;

    $resultdom = new DOMDocument();
    $resultdom->loadXML($result);

    $expecteddom = new DOMDocument();
    $expecteddom->loadXML($expected);

    $this->assertEqualXMLStructure($resultdom, $expecteddom);
}
```

Testing the REST Server Response

In our next example test case, available in `tests/customs/RESTtest.php`, we test whether the HTTP response code received is actually 200 ('OK'), as we expect:

```
class RESTTest extends PHPUnit_Framework_TestCase
{
    public function testClientCall()
    {
        $client = new Zend_Http_Client('http://zfws/rest/orders/apikey/');
        $response = $client->request();
        $this->assertEquals(403, $response->getStatus());

        // key should probably be a test key
```

```
    $client = new Zend_Http_Client('http://zfws/rest/' .
                                    'orders/apikey/oon4Choh');
    $response = $client->request();
    $this->assertEquals(200, $response->getStatus());
  }
}
```

This can be elaborated further; we could test various DELETE, PUT and POST requests and test for the response codes for every test executed. Just remember the setUp() and tearDown() should be used to prepare the underlying database for these tests, and to do some cleanup afterwards.

A wide variety of unit tests can be created, be it for the underlying libraries and models, or code interacting with the web servers, from the client or server perspective. It is time-consuming indeed, but subsequently having the ability to re-run tests quickly and easily is rewarding.

Some random notes we did not mention before that you may find interesting:

- Some IDEs allow you to start a test straight from their GUI: you should check the documentation for the IDE you use to see if and how it supports PHPUnit integration.

- If for some reason you do not like PHPUnit, there is an alternative: Simpletest[4].

- There exists another approach for creating unit tests in combination with application code, Test Driven Development (TDD). TDD tells you to write tests first and code afterwards. See Wikipedia[5] for a definition and some more information.

- SoapUI allows you to create unit tests against web services using a graphical interface. This might be of interest if you are hesitant to hand-code your tests but still want some automated tests for checking consistent behavior of your web services.

- Zend Framework itself is fully unit tested. Just download the full package from the Zend Framework's website and you will have access to the accompanying

---

[4] http://www.simpletest.org
[5] http://en.wikipedia.org/wiki/Test-driven_development

unit tests. Studying the way they are created may help you mastering unit testing.

One last thing we did not mention before: we ran each test case manually by passing it as an argument to the `phpunit` command. You can use an XML configuration file like this instead:

```
<phpunit bootstrap="TestHelper.php" colors="true">
    <testsuite name="ZFWS Test Suite">
        <directory>./application/controllers</directory>
        <directory>./application/modules</directory>
        <directory>./custom</directory>
    </testsuite>
</phpunit>
```

What this says is:

- the `*Test.php` files recursively found in the three directories should be run and
- some helper code bootstrapping some MVC parts: if you use Zend_Test this can be added in `TestHelper.php`. You are able to combine custom PHPUnit tests cases and Zend_Test-based ones that focus more on the MVC flow.

Many more configuration options are possible, the example XML configuration file listed is a very limited example, but it does allow you to just run phpunit without optional switches from the command line:

```
zfws@zfws:/web/zfws/tests$ phpunit
.......

Time: 1 second, Memory: 10.50Mb

OK (7 tests, 24 assertions)
```

Summary

- We walked through a general overview of unit testing and the use of PHPUnit.

- We tried out a few examples, creating some basic tests of our code. Many more tests can and should be created to increase test coverage.

Deliverables:

- A few basic tests were added to test the customer's web services.

Chapter 11

Security

Introduction and Background

Security and the use of techniques that might avoid abuse of online applications should be on every developer's list when planning and implementing a specific piece of code. We are not going to sum up every potential way of being hacked, as the subject is far too extensive to treat in just a single chapter. We will however repeat a few of the recommendations that can be found in the PHP manual and online authorities like Zend's Developer Zone[1], and see how we can integrate these into our previously created solutions.

Implementing security measures is something you should consider from the start, by filtering and validating user input and escaping output. The mantra "filter input, escape output" is often heard and basically means: do not trust user input, filter and apply certain restrictions on what kind of data you trust. Validate, against known rules, whatever you might expect from incoming data. Escaping output affected or potentially coming from users before displaying them in (X)HTML format is also a must.

By way of an example, posts on a forum should be handled with great care, as these kinds of public places are often used for placing pieces of JavaScript code -

---
[1] http://devzone.zend.com

JavaScript code that could, for example, take cookies from your browser and post them to remote places. This type of attack is called Cross-Site Scripting or XSS.

Another type of exploit is Cross-Site Request Forgery or CSRF. Suppose you have visited a site where you were logged in, and on that site you could order an item by simply clicking a link. Browsing away without logging out may lead you to another website that could link to the order URL, for example from within an image tag (`<img>`). You would hardly notice this, since this GET call coming from your browser is actually resulting in nothing being displayed on the page you are looking at, while an order is placed on your behalf.

The two types of abuses being mentioned are caused by misplaced trust, on the part of the user, in a website he or she is visiting or by misplaced trust a website has in a user who has already been authorized. The abuse originates from a third party however that had intent of using that implicit trust, most likely for their own benefit. The order you placed without knowing, might for example be shipped to a different address.

Direct attacks are possible too, where data sent to the server is manipulated in such a way that it:

- may become too large for the code on the web server too handle efficiently. Timeouts may occur, resulting in unresponsive websites.

- is deliberately sent in a wrong format, on which the code on the server may choke

The above may be done to make the code on the server die with an onscreen error in the hope that sensitive information (like a database connection string) may be shown as debug information. On the other hand, those kinds of attacks may be even more brutal, just aiming to bring the servers to their knees.

Repetitive requests coming from a single source (Denial of Service) or multiple sources (DDoS or Distributed Denial of Service, by a botnet of home computers infected with a computer virus for example) may lead to website outages and a loss in sales or ad revenue. Even large website infrastructures have been successfully attacked using these DDoS techniques.

Countermeasures

How to avoid these attacks and abuses? Many of the more general recommendations with regard to building secure applications apply to web services too. There is a multitude of things you can do and we will highlight just a few of them here:

Use a Firewall

With the help of a firewall, a dedicated device for example, you can block unwanted requests or request coming from unwanted source IPs. This simple countermeasure can be of great help already. Some firewall solutions even allow you to check both incoming and outgoing data for unwanted and known abusive patterns.

Combined with Intrusion Detection Systems (IDS), such as the Open Source tool, Snort, firewalls can become even smarter. Snort can detect patterns and dynamically add rules to a running firewall for blocking remote clients that show suspicious behavior. This is not for the faint of heart to configure, but it works.

Use Additional Apache Modules

Apache has an optional module named "mod_security" (ModSecurity) that acts as an intrusion detection tool at the web server level, and blocks unwanted and suspicious looking requests. You should be aware that enabling this will add some additional load on your web server however.

There also exists a patch for PHP's core functionality called Suhosin (www.hardened-php.net). This patch will help to close potential holes for abuse in PHP's internals. Some Linux distributions enable this patch by default, so check the `phpinfo()` output of your installation to see if your system is using it.

Check your Web Server

You should closely check your web server's configuration: for example, which modules are enabled, and do you actually need all of them? Do you use a shared server and are permissions on the files you published to that server permissive enough that every other user on the server can read your files? Are other tools running on the server such as forum software that has a known history of security issues?

Is other software like an FTP server running on the server and are they configured securely too?

Have a look at the online Apache manual for example, there is plenty of information available online for securing your setup.

Check and Adapt Your Code

Logging can easily be added to our web service code, not only logging accesses on the web server, but also logging of requests and responses might help you detect patterns in usage of your web services. We already showed some examples in the previous chapters on how to achieve this.

The use of blacklists and rate limiting the number of requests coming from a single source IP can be added to your arsenal of countermeasures too. Just remember that some of these IPs should possibly allow more accesses then others, since large company networks and universities for example may use just a single gateway for their internal users to browse the web.

We know how to manipulate incoming requests like we did when checking for API keys, but additional checks can be added before handing the request over to the web service, for example checks for:

- the string length of the request, imposing a maximum
- the correct format; Is the incoming request actually JSON or XML for example? Isn't it empty?
- character encoding of the request; UTF-8 could be enforced for example

PHP has the relatively unknown `filter` extension that allows for validating incoming data, for example an incoming IP or e-mail address. It also allows for defining your own callback functions to be used for filtering incoming data.

Storing incoming data should be done with great care too, using escape functions like `mysql_real_escape_string()` and prepared statements wherever possible.

Securing Communication

Just as many, many websites containing confidential information do, we could just use HTTPS instead of HTTP for our web service solutions. This basically means

HTTP using SSL for encryption of the data. If PHP is compiled with SSL (again, check your `phpinfo()` output), then you have support for HTTPS in your client side code like `SoapClient` too.

You can create a local vhost used for testing, using a self-signed certificate, and some Linux distributions even come with a ready-to-use Apache vhost listening on port 443.

Combined with an authentication scheme based on a user/password combination or an API key, HTTPS provides you with sufficient protection and a generally accepted solution for securing traffic to and from your web service.

One Step Further

You could take things one step further, and create a custom solution for example, encrypting request and responses using a public-private key solution; but in the end you have to ask yourself if all the extra effort is worth the data you are protecting using such a tedious approach.

The SOAP protocol has an extension, WS-Security. This extension allows for, among other things, encrypting the messages being sent and received. There is no WS-Security support in PHP, or in Zend Framework. In case you are required to use a WS-Security based approach, have a look at WSO2 (www.wso2.org): it offers an alternative SOAP extension for PHP with support for WS-Security. This extension is not easy to install however, nor is it easy to plow through the documentation on their site.

Besides WSO2, there exists an ongoing initiative[2] aimed at implementing WS-Security features in PHP which looks promising. Future versions of Zend Framework might have support for WS-Security in Zend_Soap, but that remains to be seen.

If you consider taking this route, be aware that it will add additional overhead to your SOAP stack (already bloated according to some) and that WSO2 itself is not straightforward to install.

Protecting communication using SSL and a hard-to-guess API key, and then enforcing the use of a unique username and password combination might be sufficient enough for most use cases, and is easy to implement and widely accepted as standard practice.

---

[2] http://code.google.com/p/wse-php

Summary

- We highlighted some of the potential problems concerning security of our web service.

Deliverables:

- A checklist of items against which to verify our web service code

Chapter 12

End-User Documentation

Introduction

If you are reading this book, you are most likely a developer yourself. Explaining the need for good documentation to a developer may be redundant, but let us give it a shot.

Web services are created for being consumed by other developers. These colleagues will appreciate good documentation, and hence this will add to the success of the API we just created. More success for the API means a happy customer. A happy customer, well, you get the point.

Good documentation also avoids support calls that will end up on your desk sooner than you would like, so it is in your own best interest too.

So why do many services and APIs have lousy documentation? Admittedly, most of us just hate writing verbose documentation for each and every class and method. Let us try another approach, one that even allows for keeping the documentation up-to-date with the code. Let us use "Reflection".

PHP's Reflection tools can be used to discover information about functions, methods, classes and even docblocks, all from existing code. Even better, let us use `Zend_Reflection` which gives us a nice and clean wrapper around PHP's built-in Reflection functionality. `Zend_Reflection` and the information contained in the docblocks will allow us to create a dynamic and continually up-to-date manual.

For this purpose, we added a new module to our application, *docs*. Inside the new modules controller directory, the `Docs_SoapController` class is added:

```
class Docs_SoapController extends Zend_Controller_Action
{
   public function indexAction()
   {
      $filename = APPLICATION_PATH . '/../library/Mta/Service.php';
      include_once($filename);
      $reflect = new Zend_Reflection_File($filename);

      $classes = $reflect->getClasses();

      if (isset($classes[0])) {
         $this->view->methods = $classes[0]->getMethods();
      }
   }
}
```

The `Mta_Service` class is included in order for Reflection to be able to read and interpret the information. Once that is done, the path to the file containing the class is given as the constructor argument of `Zend_Reflection_File`. This is part of the Zend_Reflection component and returns an object containing all information retrieved from the code. Actually, what `Zend_Reflection_File` does is quite unique, since it detects all kinds of information within the file and extracts information about required and included files, and even multiple classes can be read from the file.

The call to `getClasses()` returns an array of `Zend_Reflection_Class` instances, and since we know there is only one class in our `Mta/Service.php` file, we then get the method information from the first class found. `Zend_Reflection_Class` extends PHP's ReflectionClass and the `getMethods()` method of `Zend_Reflection_Class` returns an array of `Zend_Reflection_Method` objects. This array of objects is passed to the view. Note that `Zend_Reflection_Method` extends PHP's ReflectionMethod class.

Inside our view script, we loop over the information and prepare it for display in the view:

```
<h3>SOAP</h3>
   <div class="details">
   <?php
   foreach ($this->methods as $method) {
```

```php
      $methodname = $method->getName();
      if (substr($methodname, 0, 2) !== '__') {
         echo '<h4>' . $methodname . '( ';
         $parameters = array();
         $params = $method->getParameters();
         foreach($params as $params) {
            $parameters[] = (string) $params->getName();
         }
         echo implode(", ", $parameters);
         echo ' ) </h4>';
         echo '<div class="desc">';
         echo $method->getDocblock()->getShortDescription() . '</div>';
         $tags = $method->getDocblock()->getTags();
         $paraminfo = array();
         $returninfo = '';
         foreach ($tags as $tag) {
            if ($tag->getName() == 'param') {
               $paraminfo[] = $tag->getVariableName() .
                              ' (' . $tag->getType() . '): ' .
                              $tag->getDescription();
            } elseif ($tag->getName() == 'return') {
               $returninfo = $tag->getType() . ' ' . $tag->getDescription();
            }
         }
         echo '<div class="params">Parameters: <span class="paraminfo">';
         echo implode('</span><span class="paraminfo">', $paraminfo);
         echo '</span></div>';

         echo '<div class="return">Returns: <span class="returninfo">';
         echo $returninfo;
         echo '</span></div>';
      }
   }
?>
</div>
```

This particular piece of code will not win a beauty contest, but I am sure you get the point. What happens is this:

- we loop trough the methods and check if they do not start with "__"

- then we get the method's name, parameters and docblock and parse and output everything in a more or less structured manner.

The end result is depicted in Figure 12.1. This is a quick and easy way to build the documentation for the RPC-based services and the only thing we need for this is a short description in the docblock of each method. This will only require a small amount of effort compared to manually compiling documentation and manually synchronizing it with each change in the code.

Note that the output could be cached of course, to avoid re-reading the information from the code on each and every request.

MTA API Documentation

available services:

- SOAP
- REST
- XML-RPC
- JSON-RPC

SOAP

some information on using the SOAP server, example code maybe

getCatalogue(customer_id, category)

Returns a list of products for the customer

Parameters:
$customer_id (int): customer identifier
$category (int): (optional) category

Returns: array|object

Figure 12.1

For our REST service, we can do something similar, looping over all controllers of the REST module and printing out the gathered information.

A `Docs_RestController` class like the following can be added:

```
class Docs_RestController extends Zend_Controller_Action
{
    public function indexAction()
    {
        $controllers = scandir(APPLICATION_PATH . '/modules/rest/controllers');
        $info = array();
        foreach ($controllers as $controller) {
```

```
            if (substr($controller, -14) == 'Controller.php') {
                $filename = APPLICATION_PATH
                          . '/modules/rest/controllers/' . $controller;
                include_once($filename);
                $info[] = new Zend_Reflection_File($filename);
            }
        }
        $this->view->info = $info;
    }
}
```

The controllers in the "rest" module's controller directory are read one-by-one using Zend_Reflection_File, and the resulting array is assigned to the view script. Inside the view script, we could cycle through the information array:

```
$restaction = array('getAction',
                    'indexAction',
                    'putAction',
                    'deleteAction',
                    'postAction');

foreach ($this->info as $info) {
   $classes = $info->getClasses();

   if (isset($classes[0])) {
      $classname = $classes[0]->getName();
      $methods = $classes[0]->getMethods();
      echo '<p>' . str_ireplace(array('Rest_', 'Controller'),
                                array('', ''), $classname) . '</p>';
      foreach ($methods as $method) {
         $methodname = $method->getName();
         if (in_array($methodname, $restaction)) {
            echo '<p class="action">' . str_ireplace('action', '', $methodname)
                 . '</p>';
         }
      }
   }
}
```

The result would be very rudimentary, like the information gathered from the Rest_CustomersController class:

```
Customers
    index
    post
    get
    put
    delete
```

Output should be refined and docblock information for each method should result in verbose explanation of what POSTing to /rest/customers/ will result in, for example. The example code should point you in the right direction.

We could further expand the documentation we created. For example we could add support for multiple versions of the services (1.0, 1.1 and so on). We could even generate a small piece of sample code for every method, based on the parameter and return value information gathered using Zend_Reflection.

The error and response codes used throughout the different web services should be listed too, along with a few words explaining them.

We could also add the possibility for each consumer of our API to log in with a username and password, and eventually display the methods and resources their API key grants them access to.

All this combined would result in great documentation, which in turn would benefit you, other developers and the customer whose API you constructed.

Note that we could alternatively have used the WSDL file to create a verbose overview of methods and request and response formats allowed for the SOAP service. Converting it using XSLT (a style sheet solution for XML) for example could have helped us out.

Summary

- We explored a simple solution for creating always up-to-date documentation.

Deliverables:

- Documentation for developers interested in MTA's API

Chapter 13

Conclusion

All the combined information in this book should give you enough pieces of the puzzle to finish a project like the one we used as an example. Sure, you will do some more Googling and reading, but a lot of the basics you need for starting, designing and running a web service were at least touched upon, and some were explored in great detail.

The example code accompanying this book is far from finished so you could choose to finish that or just absorb and apply what you might have learned in your everyday job.

Keep in mind that the examples and solutions mentioned were never meant to be pictured as *the solution*, more like *a solution*. Every piece of code mentioned inside this book has at least a few other approaches that will lead you to a decent solution. Just keep an eye on the specific requirements you have for your project and hopefully you can use some of the information we explored together.

There is always more than one way to do things, but in the end it is the result that matters.

Chapter 14

Appendices

Appendix A: Development Environment Setup

A list of online resources and necessary software

Links

Software is available from these URLs. Please consider the use of nearby mirrors when downloading large packages such as Linux distribution images.

- CentOS: http://www.centos.org
- Debian: http://www.debian.org
- Fedora: http://www.fedoraproject.org
- Ubuntu: http://www.ubuntu.com
- Apache: http://httpd.apache.org
- MySQL: http://www.mysql.com
- PHP: http://www.php.net
- Zend Framework: http://framework.zend.com

For Apache, MySQL and PHP: it is probably a good idea to stick with the version supplied by your OS of choice. Zend Framework requires a PHP version of 5.2.4. Visit the Zend Framework Requirements[1] page for a detailed list of requirements.

Linux

On the platform of choice for professional developers, installation of necessary services can be done using your package manager, for example using the `apt-get` command on Debian and Ubuntu, and `yum` on CentOS and Fedora. Besides installing from packages, you always have the option of compiling everything from source. This is not always an easy route to take, particularly if you are planning to be up and running as quickly as possible. We're not going to cover that scenario here, since many online resources can get you up and running by accomplishing this if you really wish.

There are alternatives to manual installations, like all-in-one packages and scripts, such as XAMPP for Linux, that take a lot of the work out of your hands. Installing by hand however, really isn't such a drag as it might sound. Running a few commands is all there is to it.

Some distribution-specific notes and remarks follow.

Debian/Ubuntu

For Apache and PHP installation, simply run:

```
apt-get install php5 php5-cli apache2 php-pear php5-curl php5-dev
```

If you want MySQL, do this:

```
apt-get install mysql-server-5.1
```

The install script will prompt you for a MySQL root password. Optionally, and depending on your Ubuntu version, you should try `mysql-server` instead of `mysql-server-5.1` as the server package name.

---

[1] http://framework.zend.com/manual/en/requirements.html

You can also install phpMyAdmin by running `apt-get install phpmyadmin`. Once installed, the tool will be available at `http://127.0.0.1/phpmyadmin`.

Apache's default document root is at `/var/www/`, and the configuration files can be found in `/etc/apache2/`. Typically, you create an additional VirtualHost in `/etc/apache2/sites-available/newhost-name` and enable it with `a2ensite newhost-name`. Reload Apache using `/etc/init.d/apache2 reload`, and you're done.

Fedora

As an example of an RPM-based Linux distribution, here are the steps for installing on Fedora Linux:

```
yum install mysql mysql-server
```

This will install MySQL client and server packages. You'll need to activate it as a service, start it and set a password:

```
chkconfig --levels 235 mysqld on
/etc/init.d/mysqld start
mysqladmin -u root password <yourpass>
mysqladmin -h localmachine.localdomain -u root password <yourpass>
```

Install PHP and Apache:

```
yum install httpd php-mysql php-pear php-xml php-xmlrpc php-soap
```

Apache's default document root is `/var/www/html/` on Fedora, and the configuration files are here in `/etc/httpd`.

Optionally install phpMyAdmin:

```
yum install phpmyadmin
```

CentOS

Centos and Red Hat typically are a few versions of PHP behind. You can fix that by using additional repositories like the EPEL[2] and Remi[3] repository.

You'll need to install and enable the Yum Priorities package for correctly enabling these extra repos.

Rpmforge, another very popular resource for additional RPM packages, has some reported conflicts with EPEL. Don't forget to do your own research, because this may have changed by the time of publishing this book.

Mac OS X

Mac OS X users can try to tweak and customize the onboard Apache web server, but most developers choose to use a tool like MAMP[4] or XAMPP[5] for Mac OS X. Both come in free flavors and are suitable enough if it's your first dabbling in PHP on a Mac.

Windows

Since a considerable part of the PHP developer community still prefers Windows as a main development platform, I have to mention it here. XAMPP is an excellent package for development on a Windows machine. Some even use this on a production environment. It comes complete with MySQL, PEAR, plenty of PHP extensions, some onboard tutorials and many more add-ons. Use this, you won't regret it. Latest versions have PHP 5.3 support, by the way.

XAMPP supports Windows 2000, 2003, XP, Vista, and 7, and you can choose to install using an installation wizard or a zip archive where you can place (and upgrade) everything by copying it to the right location on your disk.

It is worth noting that you can also install VMWare player or VirtualBox and use a locally-running Linux-based virtual machine as your web server.

---

[2] http://fedoraproject.org/wiki/EPEL
[3] http://blog.famillecollet.com/pages/Config-en
[4] http://www.mamp.info
[5] http://www.apachefriends.org

PHPUnit and Friends

You can install PHPUnit using PEAR (for XAMPP on Windows: just at the binary directories where the `PEAR.bat` file is located to your PATH for this to work):

```
pear channel-discover pear.phpunit.de
pear install --alldeps phpunit/PHPUnit
```

While you're at it, install another handy tool, PhpDocumentor:

```
pear install PhpDocumentor
```

More information can be found on the Pear[6] and Pecl[7] websites.

Memcached

If you're planning to use and play with memcache to test some of the performance tips, install memcached using:

```
apt-get install memcached
```

You can use `yum` too, if you're on Fedora for example. Configuration of memcached can be tweaked in `/etc/memcached.conf`.

Optionally, if you're on Debian/Ubuntu and you are experiencing troubles with PHP using Memcache calls, try this:

```
apt-get remove php5-memcache
pecl install memcache
```

You need `php5-dev` for this, probably even the `build-essential` package, and if you're installing using PECL, answer "yes" to the session handler question after issuing the `pecl` command. Otherwise you won't have the ability to use the memcache extension for session handling, in case you're interested in that.

---

[6] http://pear.php.net
[7] http://pecl.php.net

Also check if the memcache extension is enabled for you PHP setup. Check the output of `phpinfo()` to be sure.

Appendix B: Specific Tools Used

This appendix will show a selection of tools and tips to explore.

Apache mod_rewrite

One of the most common web servers in use is still Apache. Rewriting a URL can be done using the "mod_rewrite" module and entries like this in the VirtualHost container that defines the host you want to do some rewriting for.

These are the default rewrite rules used for Zend Framework MVC applications:

```
RewriteEngine On
RewriteCond %{REQUEST_FILENAME} -s [OR]
RewriteCond %{REQUEST_FILENAME} -l [OR]
RewriteCond %{REQUEST_FILENAME} -d
RewriteRule ^.*$ - [NC,L]
RewriteRule ^.*$ index.php [NC,L]
```

You can find them in the `public/.htaccess` file. The rewrite options defined here are interpreted by the mod_rewrite module. It basically says that requests for any non-existent files and directories are to be handled by `index.php`, which in turn bootstraps the Zend Framework code.

Adding these lines after `RewriteEngine On` will allow requests for `/v1.0/SOAP` to be rewritten to `/SOAP.php?v=1.0`:

```
RewriteRule ^SOAP(/?)$ SOAP.php?v=1.0 [NC,L]
RewriteRule ^v([0-9]+).([0-9]+)/SOAP(/?)$ SOAP.php?v=$1.$2 [NC,L]
```

Requests for `/v2.1/SOAP/` will be redirected to `/SOAP.php?v=2.1`. The default `/SOAP` URL will be rewritten to `/SOAP.php?v=1.0`. Have a closer look and you will see it is quite trivial to understand.

More information can be found in the Apache mod_rewrite documentation[8].

Stream Wrappers

PHP has `fopen()` wrappers that allow the standard file functions like `file()` and `file_get_contents()` to read web pages from a web or FTP server for example. Stream options can be set using stream contexts. You can let the context set an authentication header as follows:

```
$url = 'http://zfws/authtest.php';
$auth = base64_encode('zfws:zfws');

$options = array('http' => array
                        (
                          'method' => 'GET',
                          'header' => array("Authorization: Basic $auth")
                        )
                );
$context = stream_context_create($options);
$result  = file_get_contents($url, false, $context);

echo $result;
```

The `authtest.php` script that checks if you are authenticated looks like this:

```
if (!isset($_SERVER['PHP_AUTH_USER']) || !isset($_SERVER['PHP_AUTH_PW']) ||
        $_SERVER['PHP_AUTH_USER'] != 'zfws' ||
            $_SERVER['PHP_AUTH_PW'] != 'zfws') {
                header('HTTP/1.0 401 Unauthorized');
                header('WWW-Authenticate: Basic realm="Restricted"');
                die('Wrong credentials');
} else {
   echo 'Logged in';
}
```

If the server-supplied authenticated user info is available, the values are checked. If nothing is found, it will prompt for a username and password. If all went well, our script should have received "Logged in" as the result.

---
[8] http://httpd.apache.org/docs/2.1/rewrite/

Stream wrappers and contexts allow for a slew of options to be set and allow for low-level HTTP calls like posting XML requests to web services and setting the required headers.

There is a PHP ini setting that defines whether the `fopen()`-related functions are allowed to open remote files: `allow_url_fopen = On`. Some hosting providers disable it; check first if you are not sure. In that case, you need a solution like cURL.

Learn more on the Wrappers[9] and Streams[10] sections of the PHP manual.

GET, POST, PUT, DELETE using cURL

PHP has support for cURL (client URL library) functions if the "curl" extension is enabled. Visit the cURL website[11] for the function reference documentation.

By way of an example, in the next example we initiate a connection using cURL, flag it as a `POST` request, allow the response to be returned and set the `POST` fields. Finally, the call is executed, which will send the XML file in the request body. The response is available in `$data`:

```
$string = '<?xml version="1.0" encoding="UTF-8"?>';
$string .= '<request><sometag>value1</sometag></request>';
$handle = curl_init('http://www.example.com');

curl_setopt($handle, CURLOPT_POST, 1);
curl_setopt($handle, CURLOPT_RETURNTRANSFER, 1);
curl_setopt($handle, CURLOPT_HTTPHEADER, array('Content-Type: text/xml'));
curl_setopt($handle, CURLOPT_POSTFIELDS, $string);

$data = curl_exec($handle);
curl_close($handle);
echo $data;
<code>
```

Command line cURL can be used too. This command will attempt to delete an order from our basic REST server:

```
<code>
curl -X DELETE http://zfws/restserver.php?id=11
```

---

[9] http://php.net/manual/en/wrappers.php
[10] http://php.net/manual/en/context.php
[11] http://php.net/curl

The HTTP request command DELETE is set using the -X flag. You can install cURL[12] using your Linux package manager, or download it[13].

Sockets

PHP has built-in functionality for using sockets. Check the example in the manual[14] that connects to a web server and sends every part of the request using socket writes. This could be used to send data to a service too, if you like to tinker around.

Appendix C: Potential Impact of ZF Moving to 2.0

Although an official date has not yet been set at the time of writing, the end of 2011 will probably bring us Zend Framework 2.0 and, for example, the MVC components of the framework undergoing an overhaul. The current roadmap is available at the official wiki[15].

PHP 5.3-specific features like the use of namespaces will be introduced, along with features like:

- a so-called "universal" constructor: all constructor methods will accept an optional array of options or Zend_Config objects, or a combination as the first argument
- changes in the dispatch cycle of the MVC components
- eventual WS-Security support in Zend_Soap, but that remains uncertain
- a new Exception regime to ensure that all of the frameworks' components throw Exceptions that are specific enough to be useful

All of the mentioned changes may affect some parts of the example code accompanying this book, but most of these examples should be easy to adapt once it becomes clear what will and will not be introduced in Zend Framework 2.0.

---

[12] http://php.net/curl
[13] http://curl.haxx.se
[14] http://php.net/fsockopen
[15] http://framework.zend.com/wiki/display/ZFDEV2/Zend+Framework+2.0+Roadmap

We cannot foresee what will happen once the roadmap is finished, but if necessary, and possible, updates to code examples may be published by the author.